Kathy Weingarten
Editor

Cultural Resistance: Challenging Beliefs About Men, Women, and Therapy

Pre-publication
REVIEWS,
COMMENTARIES,
EVALUATIONS . . .

"**T**his book locates itself squarely in postmodern thinking, reflecting feminist and social constructionist ideas. If one wanted to read the next-step thinking in those areas of hidden and settled discourses about mothers, fathers, families; about women and how the culture determines how they view themselves; about the Other, race and gender; and the polarization that occurs in public debate, one might think one would have to search far and wide in different disciplines, professional journals, recent works in progress, or speeches at major meetings. To find all this addressed in one volume is an unimaginable treat."

Victoria C. Dickerson, PhD
Co-Director, Bay Area Family
Therapy Training Associates,
and Co-Trainer, MRI Narrative
Therapy Externship

More pre-publication
REVIEWS, COMMENTARIES, EVALUATIONS . . .

"**K**athy Weingarten's heartfelt anthology *Cultural Resistance: Challenging Beliefs About Men, Women, and Therapy* is what could be called a 'clarion collection'–a call for therapists to take up arms against the restricted words (and worlds) that seem to have come to us in our mother's milk. These articles, and accompanying commentaries, challenge the cultural discourses that keep us small and mean and sometimes harmful: crippling ideals for motherhood; terrible recipes for how to be a man; unjust prescriptions for who may have children; societal pressures that lead to crippling symptoms; loaded racial binds in which Black American women must choose between the community and their own good.

This moving book is not just about therapy but about living. Please read it."

Lynn Hoffman, ACSW
Adjunct Faculty
Smith School of Social Work
Northampton, MA

"**K**athy Weingarten has composed a fascinating collection from a luminous and creative cohort of postmodern therapists. Offering provocative resistances to conventional practices in confrontation with a wide-range of issues–from anorexia and parenting dilemmas to spiritual conflicts, racism, and political disputes–these authors offer creative solutions to daily life struggles, and enterprising alternatives for therapeutic practice. Undoubtedly, the voices of these authors and their respondents help to define a wave of the future."

Mary M. Gergen, PhD
Associate Professor
Department of Psychology
Affiliated with the Women's Studies Program
Pennsylvania State University
Delaware County Campus
Media, PA

More pre-publication
REVIEWS, COMMENTARIES, EVALUATIONS . . .

"**I**n opening up the space between people to detailed scrutiny, both social constructionism and feminist theory have focused attention on those activities in which, thoughtlessly, we can trivialize and humiliate both each other and ourselves–but in which we can also, thankfully, find opportunities to be more fully human. This important book presses these inquiries forward, not only to bring new, previously 'hidden' forms of oppression into view . . . but also to outline new methods and practices for their resistance. An altogether important volume for persons and practitioners alike."

John Shotter, PhD
Professor of Interpersonal Relations
Department of Communication
University of New Hampshire
Durham, NH

"**T**his is an important collection of essays and commentaries. Each of the pieces that Kathy Weingarten has collected in this wideranging book dares to expand the limits of how we think about men, women, families, and therapy. United by their focus on going beyond the cultural stories that can construct problems, they offer us practical and original ideas for approaching therapy, research, and political conversations as acts of cultural resistance."

Jill Freedman, MSW
Co-Director
Evanston Family Therapy Center
Evanston, IL

More pre-publication
REVIEWS, COMMENTARIES, EVALUATIONS . . .

"**K**athy Weingarten's collection of essays creates a graceful collage that disarmingly challenges therapists to examine cultural lores and practices that are often taken for granted, overlooked, and left unquestioned. This book is sure to make therapists aware of the importance of being accountable *to* and responsible *to* themselves and their clients. It is requisite reading for professional *and* personal growth."

Harlene Anderson, PhD
Director
Houston Galveston Institute
Houston, TX

Harrington Park Press
An Imprint of
The Haworth Press, Inc.

Cultural Resistance: Challenging Beliefs About Men, Women, and Therapy

ALL HARRINGTON PARK PRESS BOOKS
ARE PRINTED ON CERTIFIED
ACID-FREE PAPER

Cultural Resistance: Challenging Beliefs About Men, Women, and Therapy

Kathy Weingarten
Editor

Cultural Resistance: Challenging Beliefs About Men, Women, and Therapy, edited by Kathy Weingarten, was simultaneously issued by The Haworth Press, Inc., under the same title, as a special issue of *Journal of Feminist Family Therapy*, Volume 7, Numbers 1/2 1995, Janine Roberts, Editor.

Harrington Park Press
An Imprint of
The Haworth Press, Inc.
New York • London

ISBN 1-56023-081-9

Published by

Harrington Park Press, Inc., 10 Alice Street, Binghamton, NY 13904-1580 USA

Harrington Park Press is an imprint of The Haworth Press, Inc., 10 Alice Street, Binghamton, NY 13904-1580 USA

Cultural Resistance: Challenging Beliefs About Men, Women, and Therapy has also been published as *Journal of Feminist Family Therapy*, Volume 7, Numbers 1/2 1995.

© 1995 by The Haworth Press, Inc. All rights reserved. No part of this work may be reproduced or utilized in any form or by any means, electronic or mechanical, including photocopying, microfilm and recording, or by any information storage and retrieval system, without permission in writing from the publisher. Printed in the United States of America.

The development, preparation, and publication of this work has been undertaken with great care. However, the publisher, employees, editors, and agents of The Haworth Press and all imprints of The Haworth Press, Inc., including The Haworth Medical Press and Pharmaceutical Products Press, are not responsible for any errors contained herein or for consequences that may ensue from use of materials or information contained in this work. Opinions expressed by the author(s) are not necessarily those of The Haworth Press, Inc.

Library of Congress Cataloging-in-Publication Data

Cultural resistance : challenging beliefs about men, women, and therapy / Kathy Weingarten, editor.
     p. cm.
Includes bibliographical references.
ISBN 1-56024-748-7 (alk. paper).–ISBN 1-56023-081-9 (alk. paper)
    1. Feminist therapy. 2. Constructivism (Psychology). 3. Postmodernism. I. Weingarten, Kathy.
RC489.F45C85 1995
616.89'0082–dc20
                                      95-24929
                                      CIP

INDEXING & ABSTRACTING

Contributions to this publication are selectively indexed or abstracted in print, electronic, online, or CD-ROM version(s) of the reference tools and information services listed below. This list is current as of the copyright date of this publication. See the end of this section for additional notes.

- *Abstracts of Research in Pastoral Care & Counseling,* Loyola College, 7135 Minstrel Way, Suite 101, Columbia, MD 21045

- *Alternative Press Index,* Alternative Press Center, Inc., P.O. Box 33109, Baltimore, MD 21218-0401

- *Family Violence & Sexual Assault Bulletin,* Family Violence & Sexual Assault Institute, 1310 Clinic Drive, Tyler, TX 75701

- *Feminist Periodicals: A Current Listing of Contents,* Women's Studies Librarian-at-Large, 728 State Street, 430 Memorial Library, Madison, WI 53706

- *Index to Periodical Articles Related to Law,* University of Texas, 727 East 26th Street, Austin, TX 78705

- *INTERNET ACCESS (& additional networks) Bulletin Board for Libraries ("BUBL"), coverage of information resources on INTERNET, JANET, and other networks.*
  - JANET X.29: UK.AC.BATH.BUBL or 00006012101300
  - TELNET: BUBL.BATH.AC.UK or 138.38.32.45 login 'bubl'
  - Gopher: BUBL.BATH.AC.UK (138.32.32.45). Port 7070
  - World Wide Web: http: / / www.bubl.bath.ac.uk./BUBL/ home.html
  - NISSWAIS: telnetniss.ac.uk (for the NISS gateway)
  The Andersonian Library, Curran Building, 101 St. James Road, Glasgow G4 ONS, Scotland

- *Inventory of Marriage and Family Literature (online and hard copy),* National Council on Family Relations, 3989 Central Avenue NE, Suite 550, Minneapolis, MN 55421

- *Mental Health Abstracts (online through DIALOG),* IFI/Plenum Data Company, 3202 Kirkwood Highway, Wilmington, DE 19808

(continued)

- *Social Work Abstracts,* National Association of Social Workers, 750 First Street NW, 8th Floor, Washington, DC 20002

- *Studies on Women Abstracts,* Carfax Publishing Company, P.O. Box 25, Abingdon, Oxfordshire OX14 3UE, United Kingdom

- *Violence and Abuse Abstracts: A Review of Current Literature on Interpersonal Violence (VAA),* Sage Publications, Inc., 2455 Teller Road, Newbury Park, CA 91320

- *Women Studies Abstracts,* Rush Publishing Company, P.O. Box 1, Rush, NY 14543

SPECIAL BIBLIOGRAPHIC NOTES

related to special journal issues (separates) and indexing/abstracting

☐ indexing/abstracting services in this list will also cover material in any "separate" that is co-published simultaneously with Haworth's special thematic journal issue or DocuSerial. Indexing/abstracting usually covers material at the article/chapter level.

☐ monographic co-editions are intended for either non-subscribers or libraries which intend to purchase a second copy for their circulating collections.

☐ monographic co-editions are reported to all jobbers/wholesalers/approval plans. The source journal is listed as the "series" to assist the prevention of duplicate purchasing in the same manner utilized for books-in-series.

☐ to facilitate user/access services all indexing/abstracting services are encouraged to utilize the co-indexing entry note indicated at the bottom of the first page of each article/chapter/contribution.

☐ this is intended to assist a library user of any reference tool (whether print, electronic, online, or CD-ROM) to locate the monographic version if the library has purchased this version but not a subscription to the source journal.

☐ individual articles/chapters in any Haworth publication are also available through the Haworth Document Delivery Services (HDDS).

CONTENTS

ABOUT THE EDITOR

Kathy Weingarten, PhD, is a Clinical Psychologist and Family Therapist who founded and directed for a decade the Family Systems Therapy Training Program at Children's Hospital and the Judge Baker Children's Center in Boston. She currently holds positions as Co-Director of the Program in Narrative Therapies at the Family Institute of Cambridge and as Assistant Professor of Psychology in the Department of Psychiatry at Harvard Medical School. Dr. Weingarten has published extensively on mothers' lives, intimacy, and social constructionist and feminist theory. Her new book, *The Mother's Voice: Strengthening Intimacy in Families*, was published by Harcourt Brace in 1994.

Introduction:
Attending to Absence

Kathy Weingarten

The essays in this Special Volume on cultural resistance all fall within the postmodern tradition. Each essay in this collection, in its own way, asks the quintessentially postmodern question, "What's *not* in this picture?" Though the methods vary by which we authors derive our descriptions of absence, we are all looking *through* what is conventionally accepted as "so" to pierce the invisible screen by which we, as members of a culture, as men, as women, and as therapists, are lulled into not seeing what is not there. To do this work, we must attend equally to what is present and what is absent, to what is allowed to count and what is discounted (Foucault, 1980).

Though not every essay spells out the overarching theoretical framework that underlies the work described, I think that each of the essays shares certain assumptions that fit within the social constructionist and feminist project, two theoretical systems that themselves fit the postmodern sensibility with more or less congruence.

There are three related assumptions of social constructionism that are relevant. First, the terms by which we understand the world are a product of historically situated interchange between people, not reflections of an objective reality outside of us that can be known through ever more accurate empirical investigations. Second, the degree to which a given understanding prevails is not funda-

[Haworth co-indexing entry note]: "Attending to Absence." Weingarten, Kathy. Co-published simultaneously in the *Journal of Feminist Family Therapy* (The Haworth Press, Inc.) Vol. 7, No. 1/2, 1995, pp. 1-5; and: *Cultural Resistance: Challenging Beliefs About Men, Women, and Therapy* (ed: Kathy Weingarten) The Haworth Press, Inc., 1995, pp. 1-5; and: *Cultural Resistance: Challenging Beliefs about Men, Women, and Therapy* (ed: Kathy Weingarten) Harrington Park Press, an imprint of The Haworth Press, Inc., 1995, pp. 1-5. *[Single or multiple copies of this article are available from The Haworth Document Delivery Service: 1-800-342-9678, 9:00 a.m. - 5:00 p.m. (EST).]*

© 1995 by The Haworth Press, Inc. All rights reserved.

1

mentally dependent on its objective validity, but on its use by a community of speakers, listeners, writers, and readers. Third, what we know and understand is shared with others and these negotiated meanings influence the actions we can take (Gergen, 1991).

It is this last assumption in particular that lines up with a feminist approach. A feminist approach is concerned with understanding how certain kinds of negotiated meanings operate to subjugate, marginalize, or trivialize certain people's experience, or conversely, allow it to be more fully represented. All of these essays address what has been pushed to the margins; all of these essays do so in an effort to pivot the center.

To do feminist, postmodern work, both theoretically and pragmatically, we must be able to identify cultural premises that constrain us and others. In my essay, I propose that cross-culturally there is a dominant discourse of mothers that falsely simplifies mothers' behavior, indeed their "essence," into good or bad aspects. Though the content of what makes a mother "good" or "bad" varies across cultures, the ubiquity of the split produces a shared dilemma for all mothers. Should mothers represent themselves accurately or acceptably? I argue that only when mothers feel that others truly want to hear what they experience will family members and therapists hear authentic maternal voices.

Terry Real's focus is on the binds fathers encounter in trying to raise their sons to be "masculine" according to conventional middle-class, white American standards. In challenging the task of fathering itself, he opens new ways for fathers, mothers, and sons to relate to each other.

Laura Benkov explores issues related to gay and lesbian parenting. Confronting dominant cultural assumptions about how to learn about gay and lesbian parents' lives, she and her interviewees become both subjects and subject matter. Refusing to be constrained by questions about gay and lesbian parenting that betray their heterosexist biases, Benkov's paper allows us to think about how we and her interviewees understand the nature of "family" itself.

David Epston, Rick Maisel, and Fran Morris challenge the ways women are forced to think about themselves and their bodies by a culture obsessed with appearance, thinness, and self-sacrifice for women. David Epston and his client Fran Morris share the chronicle of their work together in letters David wrote to Fran following their therapy sessions. The letters painstakingly display Fran's escape from a lifestyle that was literally killing her.

Using the discourse on Clarence Thomas v. Anita Hill as a case illustration, Jessica Daniel's paper presents a scholarly critique of the literature on sexual trauma in women's lives. Pointing out the absence of African-American women's lives from the pages of the most popular texts on trauma, Daniel meticulously details the large-scale historical traumas that African-American peoples have suffered, the daily micro-traumas they face, and the continual trauma of the erasure or distortion of the African-American female experience itself.

Melissa Griffith writes on a subject that has rarely been addressed in our field. Despite the fact that many therapists work with the concept that therapy is a process of co-constructing meaning, there is a curious absence of talk about clients' experiences of God. Her paper forces us to question ourselves: Can God be irrelevant to the lives of most of our clients? Do we invite clients to let us know about their experiences of God? Griffith discusses non-impositional ways for therapists to include in their conversations with clients their clients' conversations with God.

The final paper, written by the members of the Public Conversations Project, describes the origins of their work in their refusal to accept the seeming inevitability of polarized public positioning with regard to the abortion issue. Instead, Laura Chasin and her colleagues, Carol Becker, Richard Chasin, Margaret Herzig, and Sally-ann Roth imagined that family therapy techniques might be helpful in creating opportunities for more nuanced conversations. In this paper, the Public Conversations Project reports on their method and outcomes restoring many voices to the dominant two that have hitherto had a stranglehold on the public discourse on abortion. They cogently argue that resistance to the hegemony of polarized public positions fosters democracy.

Each paper describes cultural premises that constrain our lives as women, men, and therapists. But each goes further, as does the response that follows each paper. The second step is to develop an approach to resisting the hold these constraints have on our lives. As each of these essays makes clear, constraints operate in everyday, routine social practices: in relationships, in institutions and in texts (Scott, 1990). Cultural resistance, then, must also take place daily, in the way we live our lives with others.

As family therapists, we are in the privileged position of being invited into the daily lives of the clients with whom we work. Families come when their usual ways of relating to each other are no longer working acceptably. They are disequilibrated. As each of these essays makes clear, we can, as family therapists, use this opportunity to draw the widest possible circle around the distress, including in our description of the "problem" the cultural messages that are part of what constrict our client's lives, whether it is an idea about how a mother or father should be, how conversations should sound, what kind of talk is acceptable, etc. We can act to help family members find the words to create the ideas that most accurately represent their lived experience. In doing so, we will be practicing cultural resistance, an activity that I strongly believe deserves a place in every therapist's repertoire.

The construction of this volume reflects my own act of cultural resistance. First, each essay is followed by a response whose purpose is to extend not oppose the meanings offered in the preceding contribution. To borrow from the language of one of the essays, the form of this volume is meant to bring the reader into a conversation not a debate. As a field, too often the spirit of intellectual inquiry has a competitive edge; I am hoping to put generosity into our way of learning with and from each other. The responses of Laura Benkov, Virginia Goldner, Joan Laird, Peggy Penn, Elaine Pinderhughes, Sallyann Roth, and Michael White provide just this kind of generous and generative attention to the papers on which they comment.

Second, the volume does not make the usual distinction between essays that are primarily theoretical and those that are primarily clinical. Each paper presents a fresh way of thinking about ourselves, others, and the conversations we have together. The applications may be professional, personal, or both. The authors are peeling off layers from what is commonplace to reveal the oppression of the usual. Further, each paper incites and invites us to extend our thinking about the scope of our clinical work. In this way, I hope that this collection of papers will also challenge our beliefs about ourselves as therapists.

REFERENCES

Gergen, K.J. (1991). *The saturated self: Dilemmas of identity in contemporary life*. New York: Basic Books, 139-170.

Foucault, M. (1980). *Power/Knowledge*. Edited by Colin Gordon. New York: Pantheon.

Scott, J.W. (1990). Deconstructing equality-versus-difference: Or, the uses of poststructuralist theory for feminism. In M. Hirsch and E.F. Keller, *Conflicts in feminism*. New York: Routledge.

Radical Listening:
Challenging Cultural Beliefs
for and About Mothers

Kathy Weingarten

SUMMARY. Using a discourse analysis framework, I assert that mothers are constrained by cultural messages about "good" and "bad" mothering to "story" their lives acceptably, not necessarily accurately. The paper examines the toll that this takes on mothers–and their loved ones. I then present several therapeutic techniques to help mothers resist problematic elements of the maternal discourse within which their subjective experience of themselves as mothers has formed. *[Single or multiple copies of this article are available from The Haworth Document Delivery Service: 1-800-342-9678, 9:00 a.m. - 5:00 p.m. (EST).]*

I have been interested in mothers' stories for over 40 years, ever since my mother told me a story I could not understand. My mother was a marvelous storyteller, and I am sure she told me stories from the day I was born. I am sure she told me stories about cats and

Kathy Weingarten, PhD, is Co-Director of the Program in Narrative Therapies at the Family Institute of Cambridge; Assistant Professor of Psychology, Harvard Medical School; and in private practice.

Correspondence may be addressed to Kathy Weingarten at 82 Homer Street, Newton Centre, MA 02159.

[Haworth co-indexing entry note]: "Radical Listening: Challenging Cultural Beliefs for and About Mothers." Weingarten, Kathy. Co-published simultaneously in the *Journal of Feminist Family Therapy* (The Haworth Press, Inc.) Vol. 7, No. 1/2, 1995, pp. 7-22; and: *Cultural Resistance: Challenging Beliefs About Men, Women, and Therapy* (ed: Kathy Weingarten) The Haworth Press, Inc., 1995, pp. 7-22; and: *Cultural Resistance: Challenging Beliefs About Men, Women, and Therapy* (ed: Kathy Weingarten) Harrington Park Press, an imprint of The Haworth Press, Inc., 1995, pp. 7-22. *[Single or multiple copies of this article are available from The Haworth Document Delivery Service: 1-800-342-9678, 9:00 a.m. - 5:00 p.m. (EST).]*

© 1995 by The Haworth Press, Inc. All rights reserved.
7

good fairies and taxis that were really carrots waiting to be put in my "garage" mouth. I am equally sure that she told me stories about her life. However, I have no memory of any stories before the age of four when my mother told me a story that made no sense to me. It was a story about her, but it was also a story about me. Though it is only a sentence, it is my first remembered maternal story.

My mother was employed full-time as a newspaper reporter. I used to wait for her at the end of her day on my tricycle at the entrance to our apartment building door. I remember the sense of joy that I felt when I spied her rounding our corner, for not only would I get to be with her soon, but I would get to pedal away from the doorway out into the great big world of my city block, free and on my own in the space that was between the babysitter and my mother.

This world changed when I was four. My mother quit her job, we moved to the suburbs, and my mother became–albeit briefly–what was called then "a housewife." The story she told me about why this happened was very brief. She said, "I wanted to be at home with you."

Some might call this sentence an explanation not a story. But it was a story: the story she chose to share with me about why our lives had changed so dramatically. It was a story told to a young child who would presumably be thrilled that her mother wanted to spend more time with her. I was not. Hadn't she been at home with me before? Did this mean I had always to be at home with her? What *did* she mean? I remember the confusion I felt; the sense that a tissue-thin layer of unnameable and unspeakable difference had peeled off between us. The moment was riveting.

I do not think I am being fanciful to trace my interest in mothers' stories back so far, to such a short story as the one my mother told me that day. Embedded in that short impactful sentence was a longer and much more complicated tale: a tale about mothers, work and family, a story about a mother and what she loved. My mother didn't tell me this other story because she could not. She told a story assembled out of the elements available to her at that time–a story about the negative effects of maternal employment on children. She told me this story, even though it contradicted her own experience, because she had neither language nor concepts to imagine her story without seeming to violate something she deeply cared about, namely the well-being of her children. She was in an impossible bind. It has become my passion to help mothers tell the longer, more accurate versions of their stories. To help mothers untangle the binds they are in; to locate the words to create the constructs so that mothers–myself included–can share the truths of their lives.

STORY

Let me begin by clarifying what I mean by "story." We are all storymakers; making and remaking the stories of our own and others' lives. But we do so within certain constraints. Some stories in any culture become dominant stories and it becomes exceedingly difficult to tell tales that diverge (Kaplan, 1987; Laird, 1989). Cultures select versions of stories to legitimate and ones to deny, repress, trivialize, marginalize and obscure. This happens in cultures at large–that is, for example, Western Culture–and small cultures, like in-patient units and families.

I am using "story" to refer to the narrative form that a person, in this case a mother, gives to her thoughts, feelings, beliefs, and experiences. Stories may be very brief utterances, such as "Oh, my God," "Don't," "I love you," or intermediate in length, like the story a mother tells when she explains to her sixteen-year-old son why he must let her know where he is going to be when he goes out. And, of course, there are long stories, often renditions of one's life, that conform to the conventions of tragic, comic, dramatic, or romantic narratives (Gergen and Gergen, 1979).

According to Jerome Bruner, in *Acts of Meaning*, narrative requires, first, a means of "emphasizing human action"; second, a sequential or linear ordering of events or states; third, a sensitivity to what is canonical and what violates the accepted canon; and finally, a narrator's perspective or "voice" (Bruner, 1990, p. 77). It is my belief that it is the third and fourth requirement of narrative– knowledge of what fits the canon and "voice"–that is often highly problematic for many mothers. That is, some mothers are *so* sensitive to the ways their feelings and experience violate the accepted canon of "motherhood," that is motherhood as "institution," that their ability to place their lives in story form is profoundly affected. Critically, for many mothers, "voice" is affected too. A mother may silence or distort her voice in reaction to the contradictions she finds between what she believes (and others say) her experience should be, and what it simply is.

The silencing or distortion of maternal voice that I am speaking of is not the act of a solitary mother acting alone. Rather, it is a process that occurs in community, whereby some experiences are considered suitable and speakable and others are not. It is the rare mother who does not sometimes have a story that violates a central precept of how she and her community think a "good" mother ought to be, or feel, or behave. When this happens–whether it happens in or out of awareness–mothers are caught. Caught between representing themselves accurately and representing themselves acceptably.

DISCOURSE

In the last three years I have been working with the poststructuralist concept of discourse to help me understand the contexts of meaning within which mothers narrate their lives. Discourse, in common parlance, simply means speaking. I am using the word discourse in a more specific way. I am referring to the poststructuralist concept of discourse which social historian Joan Scott defines as a "historically, socially, and institutionally specific structure of statements, terms, categories, and beliefs" (Scott, 1990, pp. 135-136) that are embedded in institutions, social relationships, and texts. Some discourses are dominant and others are marginalized through the operation of these mechanisms. This meaning of discourse allows us to make sense of what Jerome Bruner calls the ways "culture forms mind" (Bruner, 1990, p. 24). At the same time, it is important to remember that we live in multiple cultural contexts simultaneously, and that the discourses that influence us reflect that multiplicity of cultures within which we live.

Discourse works through language and through language it shapes what we can know. In fact, a radical view of discourse holds that our conscious and unconscious thoughts and emotions, our sense of ourselves in the world, and our ways of understanding our relation to the world are constituted through language and discourse (Weedon, 1987, p. 32).

We are never subject to just one discourse. We are always subject to a multitude of discourses every day though we may not recognize them as such. Nor are discourses necessarily discrete. The discourse of mothers is inextricably connected to other discourses, for instance, the discourse of children, fathers, wives, sexuality, intimacy and many more.

A discourse may be so familiar to us that we cannot distinguish the messages that we are getting. Whether we are aware of a discourse or not, it can powerfully shape the stories we can tell and the stories we can hear. The discourse of sexual abuse provides a clear example of this for clinicians. Up until twenty years ago, therapists operated within a discursive community that made it very difficult to "hear" stories of sexual abuse. Instead, therapists often "heard" stories of hysteria. Today, it is hard to imagine a therapist who wouldn't recognize and acknowledge a sexual abuse narrative told by a distraught client.

Returning to Joan Scott's definition, she mentions that discourses are *embedded* in texts, relationships, and institutions. I want to give you an example of each of these so that you can appreciate the specificity of the word embedded. I'll start with text.

Awhile ago, I wrote a review of Jane Lazarre's *Worlds Beyond My Control* and Amy Tan's *The Kitchen God's Wife* for a professional publication. In the review I suggest that these two books provide an explanation for the writer Tillie Olsen's observation that the "voice of the mother is the largest absence in literature" (Olsen, 1978). In both books the main characters, who are mothers, silence their voice. Lazarre's protagonist literally takes a vow of silence, so certain is she that the intensity of her feelings will harm her teenage son (Lazarre, 1991). The mother in Amy Tan's novel withholds her life story from her daughter for fear that it will damage her (Tan, 1991).

In my review, I wrote "Though it is discouraging to hear this message, it is important to take it seriously. Mothers still suffer from a maternal discourse that holds them responsible for the fate of their children and simultaneously renders them powerful enough to harm them but powerless to protect them." I go on to ask, "Why can't the novelist have the mother, and why can't mothers, just speak?" In Tan's novel, I say, "the answer is the same as it is in Lazarre's: what mothers have to say can hurt children." I then go on to ask about the discursive contexts within which maternal silence makes sense, suggesting that "Mothers don't speak because what is done to mothers is unspeakable," referring, in the context of these two novels, to emotional, physical, and sexual abuse (Weingarten, 1991, 55-56).

Imagine my surprise then when the highlighted sentence in the review was the following: "What mothers have to say can hurt children." I think that this is a perfect illustration of Scott's point that dominant discourse is embedded; in this case, in text. The editorial staff, unwittingly I'm sure, selected the one sentence in the review that sustains the very maternal discourse the review is written to critique.

Two short examples will illustrate the other two arenas in which Scott believes discourse gets embedded, relationships and institutions. Every time a teacher says to a child whose family structure the teacher does not know, "Take this paper home and have your mother sign it," the teacher is embedding–that is expressing and perpetuating–a dominant discourse of "mothers are responsible for children" in her conversation with her pupils.

Finally, a California Court of Appeals ruled in 1991 that genes determine motherhood, becoming the first appellate court anywhere in the world to rule on the definition of motherhood. In the particular case, the court ruled on the request of a woman who had carried the fertilized egg and sperm of a married couple to a term birth to be declared the baby's "natural" mother and to be allowed visitation rights. The Judge declared that as the "gestational" carrier of the child, the young, single woman was merely a "host" and had no legal standing to the child (Annas, 1992). In this example, a dominant discourse about what constitutes an appropriate mother–a married versus a single one–no doubt influenced the Judge's thinking in this case.

I hope that these examples make it clear that my point is not whether a dominant discourse is positive or negative for mothers– and their loved ones, for that matter–but that discourses influence what we can know and not know, see and not see, say and not say in complex and subtle ways. As a clinician, I have developed an interest in helping mothers–myself and others–identify the particular discursive contexts which shape ways of being in the world.

I'd like to share two stories that I think are typical of the kinds of stories I hear; stories that permit the kind of investigation of discourse that I think is so helpful. These stories are short and partial. As you read them, you too will be involved in your own storymaking process about them. I would like to ask that you read these stories trusting that I am not in favor of privileging mothers' stories over children's, or father's for that matter. I invite you to read these stories in the spirit of "both/and"; in the belief that it is possible and desirable for mothers to articulate their subjective experience without burdening or harming children. That, in fact, inappropriate "dumping" or "parentifying" of children–which I certainly deplore, both for its negative consequences on children and mothers alike–is *more* likely to happen when mothers feel that they must conceal their subjective experience from their children.

These two stories have at their core maternal stories that are emblematic of the kinds of maternal stories that do not get told. Nor can I tell the maternal story itself. Rather, I can only tell the story of the therapies in which the maternal story that is there to be told has been brought forth.

SUE'S STORY:
SILENCING TO "PROTECT"
A CHILD FROM ONESELF

Sue is the mother of a three-year-old daughter, Rebecca. She and her husband first came to see me when their first-born and only child Sam was diagnosed with a terminal illness at two years of age. I worked with them through that illness and death and then through the pregnancy and birth of Rebecca, at which time they took a break from therapy because, as Sue put it, she could not feel merged with Rebecca and speak about her grief over Sam.

I have met with them in various combinations for the last year. They come because Sue is chronically depressed and there are strains in the marriage. They have done their best to answer Rebecca's questions about Sam–whose pictures are around the house–as simply and clearly as possible. Sue feels she is always managing sadness: sometimes she can keep it at bay and sometimes she cannot. Sue and Bob are convinced that Sue's sadness is going to harm Rebecca. The other day Sue called for an extra meeting.

"Rebecca asked me where Sam was?" she told me. "I told her he was in the cemetery. She kept on asking where in the cemetery. You know she's been there with us. So I finally told her, 'He's under a stone in the cemetery.' Later, I was worried that Rebecca wouldn't be able to handle this; that I'd done a terrible thing to tell her that Sam is under a stone. But this morning, she had another question. She said, 'Who put him under the stone?' I distracted her. There was a clown on the television and I told her to look at the T.V. I really don't know what to do."

Sue has a perspective on children that has been shaped by many experiences, not the least of which is the months she and her husband spent loving and caring for their increasingly vulnerable first child. Her belief in the vulnerability of children also comes from her childhood experiences with her own parents, parents who were not able to make Sue feel "undamaged" herself. Finally, she has selected out from the range of ideas about mothers in the cultures that have influenced her the idea that mothers are ultimately responsible for the fate of their children. This belief manifests itself in the idea that if Rebecca understood that her mother grieves the death of her first-born child, that her attention is not always with her, that this would irreparably harm her. Consequently, Sue, who is at home full-time with Rebecca, silences herself as best she can. By this, I do not mean simply, that she often falls out of speech, though this is also the case. Rather, I mean that she denies her feelings, splits them off where possible, responds to "meaningless" events in ways that are inexplicable to her, and suffers a debilitating depression that she and her husband find mysterious. "Why," they ask, "is Sue still having such a hard time?"

This anecdote is about a mother who conceals a central and vital part of who she is from her child, hoping that she can protect her child from the developmental interference she is sure would follow were she aware of her mother's pain. Sue restrains herself from sharing her experience with Rebecca. She has never said to her,

"I'm sad." She has never allowed herself to cry in Rebecca's presence when Rebecca has asked a question about Sam.

I think Sue's depression can be understood as an accompaniment to the fundamental self-division she enacts daily. For in the process of protecting Rebecca from her story, she splits herself into the "good" mother who protects and the "bad" mother from whom her child must be protected.

CONNIE'S STORY:
THE IRONY OF POWERLESSNESS

Connie's children are older. She has two teenage children who have both been hospitalized, Jane for running away and sexual promiscuity and Brian for substance abuse problems, depression and suicidality. Connie has been divorced from the children's father since Jane was one year old, and remarried to Jon for 10 years. The children call Jon their father.

I saw this family in consultation. Connie was the main speaker and she seemed eager to answer any questions I might have, but she was curiously airbrushed from the events she had to relay. The outlines of the story were familiar. She had been abused by the children's father, her family had not believed her, and he had finally left her with no money, two babies under two, and no address. They have never seen him since.

Curious, I asked Connie to whom she had spoken in detail about these early years.

"Oh, my God," she responded. "When I first met Jon, that's all I did. He was the first person who listened to me and believed me. I've spent hundreds of hours talking to Jon, to therapists–the kids and mine–I truly believe it's behind me."

"What about to the children?" I asked.

Jon and Connie looked at each other and Jon answered. "Connie hasn't said much of anything to the kids. We felt that they were too young."

Asked herself, Connie says she is uncertain whether or not she should tell her children more about her–and their–early experience. She reminds me that no therapist has ever suggested it would be useful.

An articulate, thoughtful, loving parent, she is desperate that her children are in so much pain. She is convinced that the tumult of their early life as a family is responsible for their problems today, but is afraid to tell her children what she remembers of those years for fear that she might make matters worse.

I am convinced that Connie would have told her children her story a long time ago if someone had challenged the idea that she could make things worse for them. Embedded in the idea that Connie could make things worse is a premise about maternal power that has a remarkable hold on Connie, and I think in our collective cultural imagination as well. Ironically, Connie was utterly powerless to influence her first husband's violence and abuse towards her or to arouse her family to come to her aid. Yet, it is the story of these events–and her central powerlessness–that now appears so powerful that it cannot be spoken.

Nobody has suggested to Connie that by *not* sharing her experience with her children, the children have been inadvertently disconnected from a significant part of their mother, a part from which they have much to learn. For what Connie would be sharing is not just events, but the meaning she has made of them, and the resolution she has struggled to achieve.

For both of these mothers, their stories about themselves have been constrained by their versions of a dominant discourse of mothers. Clinically, the task is first to surface the discourse of mothers that they live with and then to hold it up to scrutiny. This work can be done in many ways.

Attention to discourse, attention to discursive themes, is one way of doing this work. Therapists can listen for ways that mothers–and others–package their experience to fit within a dominant discourse when, in fact, their experience is not a good-enough fit with the ready-made, culturally available themes and constructs. In working this way, I have become poignantly aware that mothers literally lose experience if there are no words, no concepts, to hold it in place. I wish to turn now to ways a therapist can respond to and resist the hold of dominating discourses.

THERAPIST RESPONSES

First, I am trying to offer what I call "radical listening." Most voices and stories are authentic only when and where they are authenticated by respectful, accepting, listening (Weingarten, 1992, 1994). Therapists can contribute to the emergence of authentic voice or not, depending on whether they develop an authenticating stance. Principally, an authenticating stance is a welcoming one. It is non-judgmental, incapable, even, of prejudging. If, as I believe is so, mothers rarely tell the story of their lives unfiltered through the hobbling constructs of the cultures in which they live, then none of us, in fact, knows the stories there are to be told–the voices there are to be heard–when a mother feels she has freedom to create her own story.

Second, I listen to mothers to hear whose perspective informs their speaking about themselves. Too many times I hear mothers speaking about their own lives with the filter of a son or daughter. Sometimes a mother speaks about her own life from the perspective of the daughter that she herself has been or still is. In listening for this, I can ask the mother to reflect on her speaking, to see whether she is bringing forth her own story or the story others would have her speak.

Third, I listen for what is not present. Preformed storylines are constraining, but so are non-existent ones when they obliterate by obscuring lives that are richly in place. For example, ways of thinking about the lives of lesbian mothers and single mothers based on *their* experiences are weirdly absent from the dominant discourse of mothers (Benkov, 1994). Instead the dominant discourse has stories *about* these mothers that denigrate and distort their lives. These gaps in discourse can be, and I believe should be, addressed.

Fourth, I am extremely alert to the particular language–word choices–a mother makes. Discourses consist of language and therefore if we wish to understand the experience a mother is having we must attend carefully to her language. It will provide clues to the discourses that she is using to represent her experience.

Fifth, as important as words are for revealing dominant discourses, it is equally important to listen for those moments in which words fail. These are likely to represent moments in which the mother's lived experience falls to the margins of the dominant discourse. I regard these moments as particularly precious; they have the potential for inventing *what can be* at the same moment that they may capture what is or what has been. I try to give myself and/or the other the sense that we have all the time in the world to search for, try out, create, or bend language to serve the purposes of knowing and being known. The latent voice may speak the unspeakable, know the unknowable, if the voice feels welcomed. Journaling and dream work are particularly helpful in retrieving experience at the margins.

All of these clinical activities are building blocks that allow the client and therapist to understand the particular discursive environment within which the mother's subjective experience forms. At a minimum, there are neighborhood, ethnic, and religious variations on maternal discourse. By asking how a mother has come to believe what she does, feel what she does, assume what she does, together we can construct a description of the maternal discourse within which she mothers. For many mothers, a life task is to resist elements of the maternal discourse within which their subjective experience of themselves as mothers has formed.

An Exercise for Working with Mothers

The first step in resisting the hold a discourse may have on us is identifying its presence in our lives. The next step is the telling of narratives that more closely reflect one's actual experience, rather than the experiences one thinks one is supposed to have (White and Epston, 1990). The third step is anchoring these new narratives, an idea that I have been working with since my colleague and teaching partner Sallyann Roth first shared it with me.

The five clinical activities that I have described are all ones which, over time, can be effective in moving mothers–and others–through these three stages. Taken together and done well, they are likely to help someone move from received stories to experience-near narratives.

I have also found using exercises to be an effective clinical activity that can help mothers move relatively rapidly to a more accurate representation of themselves. I have found that adding role-playing to the clinical conversation can jumpstart, if you will, moving into voice.

The goal however, is not just to facilitate voice. Being known, being listened to, being understood are essential conditions for intimate interactions to occur (Weingarten, 1991). Mothers, so often socialized to know their children to be "vessels" into which their children can pour their stories about themselves, are often inhibited from reciprocating. They believe that to let oneself be known–to be in voice–violates a tenet of maternal discourse: mothers must be selfless. Though mothers may violate this tenet frequently by inappropriately spilling their experience to their children, this kind of sharing does not promote intimacy. It was my hope that I could design an experiential process by which mothers could have an experience of a gradual, controlled emergence of voice in relation to their children. I hoped that this would reassure mothers that speaking need not be harmful and that in fact it could produce the kind of intimate exchange with their children, even very young ones, that so many mothers desire and miss.

Drawing on the work of my colleagues Richard Chasin and Sallyann Roth (Chasin, Roth, & Bograd, 1989), I designed an exercise to take a mother experientially through the three steps I have just described. The exercise uses a simple psychodramatic method, though the effect of even the mildest psychodramatic form is usually powerful, for both the client and the clinician. The exercise provides mothers an opportunity to tell new narratives about their lives, and as such, the exercise itself is an act of resistance to the ways discourse can limit our speaking about ourselves.

Step 1: Describe a difficulty you are currently having with your child; an issue that periodically comes up for you about or with your child; or a dilemma that you experience in your mothering a particular child.

Step 2: Describe this same situation from your child's point of view.
  This is not a step that I invariably use. Often the mother is all too able to adopt the child's perspective; it is her own that is missing. If this is the case, I ask her to describe the situation the way a good friend of hers might who could have a fly-on-the-wall vantage point.[1]

Step 3: Associate to an issue or circumstance with a significant person in your life that feels in some way connected to the present situation you are describing. I have learned to ask mothers if there is yet another association that comes to mind.

The first association often clears the way for a more richly connected second association.

Step 4: Construct the story–explanation, conversation–you wish that person had had with you about herself/himself that would have been most helpful to you then, or now, in releasing you from the problem you are having with your child.

I then ask the mother if I may take on the role of the significant other and say back to her what I have just heard her say in that person's voice. In this step, a classic step in psychodrama, I am careful never to go beyond the story the mother has told. Though I embellish her speaking, I am trying, and I think I succeed, at not adding in *meanings* of my own. For the clinician it is like becoming an actor, embodying a role within the confines of an all-ready written script. In other words, this is the mother's story not mine.

Step 5: Now imagine yourself in a conversation with your child and share with your child what you feel might be most helpful to you and your child, now or later, in moving through the difficult time you are having with each other.

I have done this exercise with many mothers. Mothers associate to a wide range of people, though many do associate to episodes with their own mothers. I have noticed no difference in the efficacy of the exercise related to the choice of the significant other.

The variation in the tales that have emerged has been remarkable. However, the impact of the exercise seems to pivot around one central experience. When the mother takes on the role of the significant other, trying to act the way she wishes that person had acted, she becomes a more empathic version of that person than the one she had experienced. At some moment in this process, the mother is stymied, unable fully to become a more empathic version of the person without supplying an explanation *to herself* of the reasons the significant other has behaved as he or she has. It is at this moment that the mother attributes a context for the actions of the significant other. She tells a version of that person's story that makes his or her actions comprehensible in the past, and assimilable in the present. The context that the mother supplies is invariably one that she–now enrolled as the significant other–can live with.

When I then take on the role of the newly imagined person, I am a person with a fuller story and voice. The mother listens to this more complex and multi-dimensional person. The listening is apparently inspiring, for in the next step mothers invariably speak to their children differently than they ever have before.

One mother, having made the decision to protect her young son from the grief of her several miscarriages and stillbirths, found herself getting fixated on trivial matters with him, like whether his shirt was tucked into his pants when he left for daycare every morning. After going through the exercise she was able to share with him in some brief but accurate way what her experience was like each morning–she was imagining a breakfast table with five more children. She condensed her experience into the simple sentence, "Mommy has a lot on her mind that makes me sad at times, but it's not about you and I'm so glad that you're here." She felt immediately released from her excessive concern about his shirt, having brought herself more fully into the relationship.

This exercise enables mothers to speak what has previously been silenced. As one might predict, it is precisely these silenced feelings and thoughts that have contributed to the impasse with their child. This final speaking is often moving to the mothers, and always thrilling for me.

CONCLUSION

When a mother speaks to her children about herself, when a mother shares her life experience, she is challenging cultural beliefs. It is a form of cultural resistance. Within families, as any mother will attest–and any family therapist will too–listening to each other is the heart of the matter. The idealized mother is the person in the family who listens to others (Ruddick, 1989). I am proposing that all family members listen to mothers. More than that, I am proposing that all family members listen to each other. Helping a voice to be heard is truly radical listening (Weingarten, 1994).

NOTE

1. This alteration was suggested to be by Nollaig O'Reilly Bryne, MB, BCh, FRCP Mater Misericordiae Hospital, Dublin, Ireland.

REFERENCES

Annas, G.J. (1992). Using genes to define motherhood: The California solution. *The New England Journal of Medicine, 326*, 417-420.

Benkov, L. (1994). *Reinventing the family: The emerging story of lesbian and gay parents*. New York: Crown Publishers.

Bruner, J. (1990). *Acts of meaning*. Cambridge, MA: Harvard University Press.

Chasin, R., Roth, S. & Bograd, M. (1989). Action methods in systemic therapy: Dramatizing ideal futures and reformed pasts with couples. *Family Process, 28*, 121-136.

Gergen, K.J. & Gergen, M.M. (1979). Narrative and the self and relationship. In L. Berkowitz, (ed.) *Advances in experimental social psychology,* vol.21. New York: Academic Press.

Kaplan, E.A. (1987). Mothering, feminism, and representation: The maternal in melodrama and the woman's film 1910-1940. In C. Gledhill, (ed.) *Home is where the heart is: Studies in melodrama and the woman's film*. London: The British Film Institute.

Laird, J. (1989). Women and stories: Restorying women's self-constructions. In M. McGoldrick, C.M. Anderson, & F. Walsh, *Women in families: A framework for family therapy*. New York: W.W. Norton.

Olsen, T. (1978). *Silences*. New York: Delacorte Press/Seymore Lawrence.

Scott, J.W. (1990). Deconstructing equality-versus-difference: Or, the uses of poststructuralist theory for feminism. In M. Hirsch and E.F. Keller (eds.) *Conflicts in feminism*. New York: Routledge.

Tan, A. (1991). *The kitchen god's wife*. New York: G.P. Putnam's Sons.

Weedon, C. (1987). *Feminist practice and post-structuralist theory*. Oxford: Basil Blackwell.

Weingarten, K. (1991). Listening to maternal voices: Stories in context. *AFTA Newsletter*, 55-56.

_____ (1991). The discourses of intimacy: Adding a social constructionist and feminist view. *Family Process 30*, 285-305.

_____ (1992). Consultations to myself on a work/family dilemma: A postmodern, feminist reflection. *Journal of Feminist Family Therapy*, 4(1), 3-29.

_____ (1994). *The mother's voice: Strengthening intimacy in families*. New York: Harcourt Brace.

White, M. & Epston, D. (1990). *Narrative means to therapeutic ends*. New York: W.W. Norton.

Out of Objectification:
Comment on Kathy Weingarten's
"Radical Listening:
Challenging Cultural Beliefs
for and About Mothers"

Laura Benkov

There are stories we are unable to tell even to ourselves, let alone to those around us. Other stories we may know, but seal off from the people we live among. Alternatively we may try to tell stories that others fail to apprehend for a multitude of reasons. Then too there are stories that, though shared among a group, remain virtually invisible to the larger culture.

What are the costs of an untold story? As Kathy Weingarten suggests, they are many and varied. She tells us of a mother isolated in the grief she tries to shield her child from, her struggle to keep sadness at bay creating an ever widening distance between her and the child she so loves. Weingarten tells us also of a mother who sees her painful process of extricating herself from an abusive marriage as a tale that her children need to be protected from rather than as a journey from which her children might have much to learn. Confu-

Laura Benkov, PhD, is a Supervising Psychologist in the Department of Psychiatry, Children's Hospital, 2 Longwood Avenue, Boston, MA 02115.

[Haworth co-indexing entry note]: "Out of Objectification: Comment on Kathy Weingarten's 'Radical Listening: Challenging Cultural Beliefs for and About Mothers'." Benkov, Laura. Co-published simultaneously in the *Journal of Feminist Family Therapy* (The Haworth Press, Inc.) Vol. 7, No. 1/2, 1995, pp. 23-26; and: *Cultural Resistance: Challenging Beliefs About Men, Women, and Therapy* (ed: Kathy Weingarten) The Haworth Press, Inc., 1995, pp. 23-26; and: *Cultural Resistance: Challenging Beliefs about Men, Women, and Therapy* (ed: Kathy Weingarten) Harrington Park Press, an imprint of The Haworth Press, Inc., 1995, pp. 23-26. *[Single or multiple copies of this article are available from The Haworth Document Delivery Service: 1-800-342-9678, 9:00 a.m. - 5:00 p.m. (EST).]*

© 1995 by The Haworth Press, Inc. All rights reserved.

sion, isolation, emotional distance, lost opportunities to grow–these are just some of the personal costs of untold stories.

Lurking among these costs is another that is at once deeply personal and profoundly political. Perhaps the greatest cost of a story untold is the objectification of the silenced, would-be speaker. Indifference, bigotry, and violence are all rooted in such objectification. Thus finding the voices with which to tell our deepest truths and the hearts with which to apprehend the truths of others are the cornerstones of personal as well as political change. Weingarten contributes greatly to both endeavors. While there is much to be appreciated in "Radical Listening: Challenging Cultural Beliefs for and About Mothers," these are two aspects of the article that are especially vital contributions.

By now, the phrase "the personal is political," has been so oft repeated that it frequently seems to have nothing new to offer even those for whom it was a powerful rallying cry. And yet, I believe, we are only at the beginning stages of reckoning with the implications of this phrase. Steeped in a culture that is rife with dichotomous thinking about individual experience on the one hand and social forces on the other, it is often difficult to reconceptualize these seemingly discrete entities as one, and moreover, to do so in a way that has pragmatic as well as theoretical implications.

In recent years, several disciplines have begun to enter this territory. There are, for example, rich traditions in symbolic anthropology (Geertz, 1973; Rosaldo, 1984) and critical legal studies (Williams, 1991) that delineate with great specificity the ways in which we are, as individuals, fundamentally social beings. As Weingarten draws on the literature about discourse, she brings psychology into this territory, where it becomes possible to recognize the social nature of our most profound individual experiences.

Psychology is a particularly difficult discipline within which to establish this perspective. Of all the social sciences it is the one that has attended least to historical and cultural specificity, and most blatantly postulated decontextualized, universal models of human experience. Moreover, attempts to integrate political analyses into the theory and practice of therapy have often been dismissed as superficial, while psychoanalysis, practiced in the most culturally decontextualized way, has been put forth as the only road to the "depths" of human experience. Unfortunately, many attempts to integrate an analysis of social context into psychological theory have not adequately grappled with the complexity of individual lives, and thus the criticism has been at least partially well-founded. It is here, that work like Weingarten's is so crucial. By starting from the premise that multiple discourses shape what stories we can and cannot tell, Weingarten contextualizes individuals in a way that gives access to both political analyses and the most deeply felt experiences. As she guides us through the process of listening to submerged stories, attending to the discourses that shape stories, to specific word choices and to the words that are not there, Weingarten teaches us anew the meaning and possibilities inherent in the phrase "the personal is political."

The implications of Weingarten's "radical listening" are far reaching. In this article she explores only one of many instances in which the effort to resist dominant discourses is vital. Weingarten writes that she wants "to locate the words to create the constructs so that mothers . . . can share the truths of their lives." This is as radical an idea as her approach to listening. Mothers are so rarely subjects in psychological discourse. They are, instead, the objectified backdrops of their developing childrens' lives. Inherent in our inattention to mothers' stories is the idea that maternal/child relationships are a zero sum game. It is as though the telling of one story will obliterate the unfolding of the other. Weingarten challenges this zero sum thinking, suggesting instead that both mothers' and their children's lives are enhanced by attention to maternal stories. Thus she points the way to a psychology in which mothers are subjects alongside their children. She writes "If, as I believe is so, mothers rarely tell the story of their lives unfiltered through the hobbling constructs of the cultures in which they live, then none of us, in fact, knows the stories there are to be told–the voices there are to be heard–when a mother feels she has the freedom to create her own story." I would add that none of us knows what the world would be like if children grew up not only knowing these untold maternal stories, but knowing also in their hearts the process through which such stories can be told.

REFERENCES

Geertz, C. (1973). *The interpretation of cultures.* New York: Basic Books.
Rosaldo, M.Z. (1984). Toward an anthropology of self and feeling. In R.A. Shweder and R.A. LeVine, *Culture theory: Essays on mind, self, and emotion.* Cambridge: Cambridge University Press.
Williams, P. (1991). *The alchemy of race and rights: Diary of a law professor.* Cambridge, MA: Harvard University Press.

Fathering Our Sons;
Refathering Ourselves:
Some Thoughts on Transforming
Masculine Legacies

Terry Real

SUMMARY. Traditional narratives concerning the "masculization" of boys promote a variety of relational woundings, some active some passive, in the name of fathering. Some current myths about the "development of masculine identity" are deconstructed, the consequences for adult males of the emotional trauma which is an integral part of most boy's development is outlined, and a vision of relational fathering is offered as an alternative. *[Single or multiple copies of this article are available from The Haworth Document Delivery Service: 1-800-342-9678, 9:00 a.m. - 5:00 p.m. (EST).]*

A male client of mine once gave me the gift of an old Yiddish saying. I won't pretend to remember the Yiddish, but the translation ran something like this: "The son wishes to remember what the father wishes to forget." In other words, the son, in his journey to maturity, needs somehow to uncover precisely what the father, in his development as a man, felt a need to disavow.

Terry Real is on the faculty of the Family Institute of Cambridge, 51 Kondazian Street, Watertown, MA 02172.

[Haworth co-indexing entry note]: "Fathering Our Sons; Refathering Ourselves: Some Thoughts on Transforming Masculine Legacies." Real, Terry. Co-published simultaneously in the *Journal of Feminist Family Therapy* (The Haworth Press, Inc.) Vol. 7, No. 1/2, 1995, pp. 27-43; and: *Cultural Resistance: Challenging Beliefs About Men, Women, and Therapy* (ed: Kathy Weingarten) The Haworth Press, Inc., 1995, pp. 27-43; and: *Cultural Resistance: Challenging Beliefs about Men, Women, and Therapy* (ed: Kathy Weingarten) Harrington Park Press, an imprint of The Haworth Press, Inc., 1995, pp. 27-43. *[Single or multiple copies of this article are available from The Haworth Document Delivery Service: 1-800-342-9678, 9:00 a.m. - 5:00 p.m. (EST).]*

© 1995 by The Haworth Press, Inc. All rights reserved.

27

From the moment I first heard this saying I was struck with its wisdom. What is it exactly that we hungry young men seek to ferret out of our fathers? From where comes this depth of need, this grief-tinged longing? I don't know about Yiddish culture, but, for my own, I have come to believe that that which the sons so passionately wish to remember, that which our fathers have come so thoroughly to forget, is nothing more or less than the relational being, the personhood, of the father himself.

What is fathering? Is it an activity or a relationship distinct from mothering, or from parenting in general? To understand fathering in the present dominant culture, I believe we must silhouette it against the backdrop of current narratives concerning masculinity and the "masculinization" of our sons.

TIMMY

"I remember the first time Bill did it." Ann looks up at me from her chair. "Timmy was lying in my lap, just resting, and Bill simply walked over and took Timmy's hand and said, 'Come here,' and whisked him off. I didn't realize what he was doing, at first. I thought he was taking him somewhere. But then it became obvious.

"So, I said to him, 'Bill, what are you doing?' and he got very angry with me. He said, 'He's too old. You have to learn to let go of him.' And I said, 'He's just a child.' And he bent right over me, very close, very upset and he said, 'You will *not maul that* boy!' I knew, of course, that he was talking about his relationship with his own mother, but I honestly didn't know what to say. I still don't know what to say."

"So," I ask, "Have you complied? Have you left Timmy alone?"

Ann smiles mischievously. "I *sneak*," she says.

Ann's smile is so impish. Her solution has such a familiar feel, that it seems meanspirited to break with her lighthearted tone. Yet, if we step back a bit and cast a cool eye on this simple transaction, we can see that it speaks volumes about gender arrangements inside the contemporary family, and most of what it has to tell us is not good news.

Let's start by asking the same question about Bill that Ann asked. *What is he doing?*

Bill is attempting to ensure that his son is not babied, "enmeshed," drained by the "regressive" pull of his mother. Bill wishes to help his son move into masculinity by helping him loosen the maternal bond. While Bill's behavior is abrupt and extreme, what moves him is a force which is everywhere in the dominant culture. It might manifest itself in the voice of a gym teacher who mocks Timmy however good-naturedly when he's too shy to join in a schoolyard game; or in the voices of Timmy's school chums who also ridicule him for not joining in, though less good-naturedly. It is in the silence of Timmy's mother who doesn't quite know what to say to a son who tells her that he cried. Should she support his tears or his need to push through them?

THE MYTH OF "MASCULINE IDENTITY"

What underlies all of these transactions is a belief shared by many about what it means to be a man and how boys achieve manhood. That underlying belief may be summed up in the following assertion: *The establishment of a stable sense of masculine identity is essential for a boy's mental health. Such a process requires a disidentification with mother and a firm identification with father.*

Let's "unpack" some of the assumptions embedded in that assertion.

First, that such a thing as a "masculine identity" exists.

Second, that such an identity is a good thing to have.

Third, that one does not simply have a masculine identity, one needs to establish it and that, furthermore, its establishment may or may not prove "stable."

Fourth, that a critical component of the task of securing such an identity is through "identification" with one's father.

Fifth, that a corollary component of the task of securing such an identity lies in repudiating one's connection with one's mother and with the "feminine" in general.[1]

In the pioneering work on the sociology of gender in the 1970's and in the nearly two decades of research that have followed, no persuasive evidence for a single one of the above assumptions has been established (Bloch, 1978; Fein, 1977; Pleck, 1981). The terms of the many hypothesized "masculinity/femininity" scales and other such measures have been repeatedly critiqued as culturally relative (Pleck, 1981). To date no evidence has emerged to substantiate the notion that boys create a stable internal psychological structure matching the numerous descriptions of "masculine identity," or that such a stable structure is necessary for psychological health.[2]

As a classroom exercise, I have taken to reading aloud to my students lists of questions from such measures from the fifties and sixties. I have found few things as much fun or as hard to argue with regarding the relativity of our thinking about what constitutes masculine versus feminine attributes. Do you prefer a bath or a shower? Do you get excited very easily? Do you like to read mechanics magazines? (Gough, 1952; cited in Pleck, 1981). And yet, that shibboleth, unstable masculine identities–with its concomitant counterpart, absent father role models–has been blamed for everything from drug addiction to juvenile delinquency, homosexuality and murder.

The myth of the disidentification with mother and necessary identification with father wound its way from Sigmund Freud through Talcott Parsons to generations of feminist writers like Nancy Chodorow, Jean Baker-Miller, Dorothy Dinnerstein and Carol Gilligan. Coming through the triple channels of psychoanalytic theory, sociology and cultural feminism, this narrative has gained extraordinary legitimacy and is offered, with unquestioned centrality, in just about all of the current psychological literature on men (e.g., Betcher & Pollack, 1993; Meth & Pasick, 1990; Osherson, 1986). A typical example can be found in Samuel Osherson's wonderfully sensitive and useful book, *Finding Our Fathers:*

> The press to identify with father creates *the crucial dilemma* (italics, mine) for boys. Boys have to give up mother for father, but who *is* father? Often a shadowy figure at best, difficult to understand. Boys rarely experience fathers as sources of warm, soft nurturance. The most salient adult object available for the boy is his mother. . . . What does it mean to be male? If father is

not there to provide a confident rich model of manhood, then the boy is left in a vulnerable position: having distanced himself from mother without a clear and understandable model of male gender upon which to base his emerging identity." (1986, p. 6)

While Osherson renders this account with characteristic empathy and warmth, he, like many others, does not pause to question the story's basic assumptions. Why must the boy give up his mother? Why must he have a "confident rich model of manhood?" Why must he learn what it means to be male at all? Isn't he male, already? Does he need, for example to learn what it means to be two-legged, or tall? Must he labor so intently to establish a stable psychological structure concerning his identity as a redhead or brunette, an American, a Methodist, an Ohioan, a great bowler? Why are we picking out this aspect of identity and making such a fuss over it?

For several decades, researchers attempted to operationalize the concept of masculinization through identification with father through correlational research. Researchers measured "masculinity" in fathers and then in their sons to determine the presence and strength of correlation. They found no robust correlation (Biller, 1971; Lamb, 1986).

The critical variable for the development in boys of a stable sense of identity and a positive attitude toward themselves as males turned out to be, not the degree of "masculinity" measured in the father, as predicted, but the warmth of the father-son relationship (Lamb, 1986). The crucial variables seemed relational–warmth, attachment, affectation–the very qualities presumably correlated, according to traditional ideas, with the father's "femininity!"

As Lamb (1986) points out, the idea of identification with fathers was such a *given* that researchers took awhile before asking the very commonsense question, "Why should boys *want to identify* with their fathers?" Subsequent research provided an answer: boys like to be like fathers whom they like (Munsen & Rutherford, 1963; cited in Lamb, 1986). It is a testament to the sway of cultural assumptions that it took several decades to figure that out!

Another question it took some time for researchers to ask was, "What is it exactly that boys who identify with fathers identify with?" In other words, what is this manhood that fathers supposedly model? Again, the answer that emerged ran counter to researchers' expectations. As a number of investigators and writers noted, boys' and men's senses of themselves as masculine have little to do with the attainment of any positive value. Masculinity is, as Chodorow put it, "a negative achievement" (Chodorow, 1978). Boys' "emerging masculine identities" seem less about positive attributes we call masculine than they are about the repudiation of what the dominant culture deems feminine—not being girlish, not being like mother, not crying and so on. In theory, a man's identification with his father is thought to be highly significant, but when one invites boys and men to speak in depth about their masculinity, it is emphatically the disidentification with mother that most matters to them (Levinson, 1978).

TRADITIONAL FATHERING
AS PSYCHOLOGICAL VIOLENCE

When we, as fathers, clinicians, and researchers, stand clear of the embedded assumptions, it becomes apparent that our anxiety over and endless quest for masculine identity is not about furthering our sons' development, but about the imposition of role compliance through enforced repudiation. To teach our boys to become men, to father them traditionally, is to teach them, indeed to compel them, to disconnect—from their mothers, from their needs, from their soft emotional sides, from expressiveness, vulnerability, succor—in a word, from the relational domain both within and without.[3] Traditional fathering, intrinsically, structurally, inescapably, requires psychological violence.

I agree with Silverstein's (1994) observation that, in the current dominant culture, each sex is asked to halve itself. Girls and women are traditionally asked to inhibit the development and expression of public assertive agency, boys and men are traditionally asked to inhibit the development and expression of relational and affective connectedness. For decades, feminist scholars have documented both the coercion necessary to enforce role compliance and the negative psychological consequences of such compliance for women (e.g., Crowly, 1991). I believe a complimentary coercion and a reciprocal set of psychological consequences are operative for men (e.g., Connoll, 1987).

Take an utterly mundane occurrence. Janie and her sons sit at the dining room table. David, who is fatigued and somewhat depressed, joins them after a long day at the office followed by a tough commute home. Janie wants to talk–to David, to the boys–about their day and hers. David wants to "relax," that is, to be left alone. After a few abortive efforts, Janie gives up and, rather than confront David, supplements his lack of interest with redoubled efforts of her own toward the kids. The boys, particularly the oldest, pick up Dad's cue and freeze out their mother with monosyllabic responses. Janie, afraid to "infantalize," willing to give her men "their space," eventually amiably withdraws. She putters about the kitchen and cleans up while David listens to the news and the boys go off to sports or video games or homework. What has just occurred is completely, thoroughly seamless. There passes not a ripple of overt discontent. And yet, from the perspective I have gained from work with men, this simple, everyday scene is nothing short of psychologically chilling. What have these sons learned about what it means to be a man?

First, they have learned not to expect their father to attend to them or to be expressive about much of anything. They have come to expect him to be psychologically unavailable. Second, they have learned that he is not accountable in his emotional absence, that Mother does not have the power to either engage him or confront him. In other words, Father's neglect and Mother's ineffectiveness at countering it teach the boys that, in this family at least, men's participation is not a responsibility but rather something voluntary and discretionary. Third, they learn that Mother, perhaps women in general, need not be negotiated with or taken too seriously. One can, just like Dad, stonewall them. Fourth, they learn that not just Mother, but the values she manifests in the family–connection, expressivity–are to be devalued and not responded to. The subtext message is, "engage in 'feminine' values and activities and risk a similar devaluation." The paradox for the boys is that the only way to connect with Father is to join him in apparent needlessness. Conversely, being too much like Mother threatens further disconnection or perhaps, active reprisal.[4] In this moment, and thousands of other ordinary moments, these boys are learning to accept psychological neglect, to discount nurture, and to turn the vice of such abandonment into a manly virtue.

ACTIVE AND PASSIVE ABUSE

To understand the ordinary moments of psychological violence that are an intrinsic part of most boys' development, I have found it helpful to keep in mind a distinction I first encountered in the literature on trauma recovery, a distinction between what I call *active* and *passive* abuse.[5]

Active abuse is usually a boundary violation of some kind, a clearly toxic interaction. Passive abuse, on the other hand, is a form of physical or psychic neglect. Rather than a violent presence, passive abuse may be defined as a violent lack, the lack of forms of nurturance or responsibility which one might minimally expect a caregiver to demonstrate.

While passive abuse is, in all but the most extreme instances, more elusive than flagrant active abuse, my clinical work has brought me to agree with the observation that passive abuse in childhood, particularly when pervasive and covert, may cause serious impairment in later years (Janoff-Bulman, 1992; Mellody, 1989).

One of the things I have learned in working with issues of abuse over the years is that there isn't always a simple and direct correspondence between the flagrancy and severity of childhood abuse and the degree of impairment in later life. The child of a consistently psychotic parent, for example, may emerge relatively unscathed if he or she is fortunate enough to find others for nurture, guidance and the support of his or her reality testing about the sick parent. On the other hand, I have worked with people whose major caregivers looked nurturing enough overtly but who were capricious and inconsistent, whose emotional withdrawal or punitiveness was subtle and covert. That environment left my clients deeply impaired in their capacity for intimacy and impaired, furthermore, in a way that was difficult to rectify even with years of therapy.

Men's Group

In the Wednesday night men's group I have lead for the past two years, Ryan "checks in," with the tale of a "small roadside epiphany." Coming home from a party, Ryan's wife, Lilly, expressed hurt and anger at a repeated pattern in which Ryan, affectionate in private, would "disown and shun" her in public gatherings.

"She told me it felt as if I wanted to act like I didn't know her." Ryan told us. "In the past, I would have gotten defensive and probably started a fight, but this time I was so . . . I don't know, so stunned, I just pulled over on the side of the road and shut off the car." Lilly was right, Ryan realized. With a few years of therapy behind him, Ryan allowed himself to be flooded not only with the truth of her account and the pain it caused her, but also with remembered associations. Ryan's parents rarely demonstrated physical affection for one another and, while they had shown physical nurture to him as a young boy and still did to his sister, they had severed that connection with him from about the age of six or seven.

What Ryan recalled, sitting on the side of the road, was a vivid memory of himself as a boy of seven or eight, crying hysterically in the middle of the kitchen asking for a "pick up," while his family bustled around him preparing dinner as if he simply wasn't there. "It was as if my parents made a decision one day to stop, although I'm sure they didn't because they didn't talk about things like that. I don't think my father touched me again, except maybe once or twice every few years he would totally lose it and throw me against a wall. I think that was it."

I lead Ryan through a quick guided imagery exercise. I asked him to close his eyes and see himself lifting his infant son in the air and laughing together, a scene he had described many times to the group. I asked him to note the joy, the sheer pleasure in each of their faces. Then I asked him to imagine himself as a child being touched with such joy by his father. Ryan began to cry, softly, silently. "That was your birthright," I told him. "His thrill to be with you. You deserved that." Beside Ryan, George also began quietly to cry. When I asked what was triggered, he recalled that on the afternoon of his MBA graduation, his father hugged him and said he loved him for the first time in his life. "I was twenty six years old," he mused. "Even a BA wasn't enough to get it out of him. I had to earn a fucking *graduate* degree." George smiled ruefully, tears still in his eyes. "If I'm still in this damn group when I have a child, I swear I am going to tell that precious creature I care about him or her at least once a day, do you hear me? At *least* once a day. If I don't, you can drag me out of the house and knock some goddamn sense into me."

Does calling such neglect abusive trivialize the nature of abuse? I don't think so. I think not touching a child for decades at a time is a form of violence. I think withholding any expression of love until a young child is a grown man is a form of violence. And I believe that the violence men level against themselves and others is bred from just such circumstances. Ryan first came to therapy after a year of escalated alcohol abuse and several instances of hitting his fiancée. He lost the relationship but, with my help, entered treatment for his drinking and an underlying depression. When George was referred to me for a consult, he was suicidally depressed and on the verge of an emergency hospitalization. These men are not whining. These injuries are not shallow. Minimizing their distress, minimizing men's distress in general, is not merely wrong, it is dangerous.

In trade for multilevelled, pervasive abandonment, and the demand that boys learn to abandon whole parts of themselves, the dominant culture traditionally offers boys and men the recompense of privilege. We are to be catered to, we are to be waited upon, we are to be "supported." When push comes to shove, whether it's in corporate glass ceilings or in the flash of domestic violence, if men's interests are sufficiently threatened, many will allow themselves recourse to outright coercion.

Good therapy with men demonstrates with each session that the traditional *quid pro quo* is a deal with the devil. It is exactly the deal Faust struck with the marvelously seductive Mephistopheles, the trade of worlds of power and knowledge, of the capacity to *do*, in return for our very (relational) souls.

Mellody draws a distinction between abuse of disempowerment, shaming transactions, and abuse of "false empowerment," transactions which further grandiosity (Mellody, 1989). Either puffing up a child inappropriately or simply failing to limit a child's natural grandiosity is a form of abuse which leads inevitably to disorders of self-esteem. We may be unaccustomed to thinking (particularly those of us who are used to a political analysis) of inflation of ego as a form of abuse, but in terms of the requirements of good parenting such transactions are demonstrably bad for children.

The relevance of gender to the distinction of disempowering and falsely empowering abuse is important and should be obvious. Girls and women in this culture tend to be subject to abuse of disempowerment, boys and men are subject to transactions which alternate between the two. Neither leads to healthy self-esteem or a mature capacity to tolerate the vigorous negotiation of relationship.

For decades, feminist writers have shed light on the victimization of girls who are disempowered and shamed. Dare we now risk empathy for those who are falsely empowered, those who will offend others? Not only can we, but I believe that we must if we are to heal the split currently in the culture with regard to men. In my view, those of us who have held a feminist position have historically viewed men, and have used rhetoric which described men, primarily as oppressors. While such descriptions may make for good political analysis, they are an untenable language for therapy. On the other hand, traditional empathy-driven therapy, and certainly the "man-as-wounded" frame current in most of the literature coming out of the men's movement (both the mythopoetic men's movement and current books on men's psychology) woefully ignore the whole issue of privilege and oppression. Bograd (1993) has asserted the need for "a new lexicon" of therapy for men. I believe she is right and I believe that looking at issues of abuse provides an excellent alternative to the extremes of either further objectifying men in the name of politics or depoliticizing men's actions in the name of psychological understanding.

Therapeutic Implications

In therapy with men, the therapist—male or female—must simultaneously hold clients in empathy and yet still hold them accountable. Therapists must hold male clients, as Sternbach puts it, as both *wounded and wounding* (Sternbach, 1993). I believe therapy that looks sympathetically and squarely at the ways in which men are both abused and are also set up to become abusive to others offers hope for real change.

Mephistopheles, like any traditional father/mentor, offers Faust, his spiritual son, a double dose of toxicity: the abandonment of real vulnerability and relatedness which is then compensated for by grandiosity, the illusion of needlessness and privilege. It is a fountain of knowledge without wisdom which leaves the drinker thirstier than before.

The position that boys, later men, inhabit is akin to that of the "special child" (Lomas, 1967) in the narcissistically disordered family, the position of the "parentified child" (Minuchin, 1974) and the "hero" (Woititz, 1983). I have described this position as "the masochism of grandiosity" (Real, 1978). The child has inordinate power and place, but only upon condition that he abdicate his own authentic needs. In other words, I believe that a narcissistic disorder, a disorder of self, is to some degree the norm for men in our society.

Furthermore, in the very moments that we are being abjured by our fathers to "grow up," "stop whining," "break away," we are being bathed, covertly, in their grief over the very wounds inside themselves that they now inflict. The "unfinished business" (Osherson, 1986) our fathers have not attended to, the issues and feelings they have not responsibly dealt with inside themselves, are absorbed by their porous sons.[6]

For years I, quite wisely, refused to work with violent fathers. Now, I work with them often. Each time I do, I vividly recall my own father out of control in his rage, and yet my feeling, even as he lashed out, was mostly sad for him, tender. Through the tone of his voice, the quality of his touch, the pain in his eyes, my father leaked the depression he didn't know he had out onto me, and, upon occasion, like many fathers of his generation, he beat it into me with the back end of a strap.

In hindsight it is clear to me that I became a therapist so I could cultivate the skills I needed to heal my own father–to heal him at least enough to get him to talk to me. I needed enough information from him to be able to come to terms with his brutality so that I might lay my hatred of him to rest. At first I did this, quite unconsciously, not out of any great love for him, but out of an instinct to save myself. I wanted the legacy to stop.

I had to refather my father enough to allow him to at least minimally father me. In the last years of his life, we managed to do a lot better than the minimum, but that is another story. Suffice it to say that I take what I learned from that process into the task of refathering the men I work with each day. While space will not allow a detailed illustration of a variety of techniques I find helpful, I will provide a conceptualization of what refathering means.

Refathering as Parenting

To understand refathering, I must first be clear that I do not believe in the idea of fathering to begin with, any more than I believe in mothering. I do not believe in the division of life experience or the doctrine of separate spheres. I believe in parenting. I don't believe that we need bother turning boys into men or girls into women–nature will take care of that all on its own. I do believe that mature adults need to help children turn into mature adults. What this means is that mothers can show their children, both boys and girls, how to be sensitive *and* assertive. That fathers can show their children, both boys and girls, how to be competent *and* vulnerable (Silverstein, 1994).

While I do not believe that boys internalize masculinity from their fathers and other role models, I do believe that they internalize something. Among other things, I believe, they internalize contempt. The true sequelae of the abuse leveled against boys is closer to the psychoanalytic idea of identification with the aggressor than it is with the idea of role models. What the trauma and abuse literature tells us is that in moments of abuse, or, in other words, of boundary failure, predictably, the victimized child will move to protect the psychic equilibrium of the offender and will adopt the attitudes toward himself or herself that the offender has (Gelinas, 1983; Mellody, 1989). This moment of what I call "empathic reversal" lies at the heart of understanding men in our society. In such instances of abuse, either active or passive, discrete or acted out over time, the boy comes to shift his allegiance (identification, if you like) to the views and attitudes of the offender (or the contemptuous messages of the culture at large). He loses empathy with his own boyish, needy, "feminine" self and adopts empathic attunement to those who hold that self in contempt. This is the moment (or, more accurately, thousands upon thousands of repeated moments) of loss of the boy's relational self.

What all of the techniques of refathering have in common, as I use them, is a reversal of this reversal, so that empathy is reestablished for the boy in the man, and accountability is reasserted vis-à-vis the offender (whether that means the original offending caregiver, the offending messages from the culture at large, or the offensive parts of his grown-up self). This can be done through adapting a variety of commonly used family therapy techniques: for example, through role play experiences in which parts of the self may be extracted, acted out, modified; or through family of origin work, either by letter, role play, or with the adult male's actual parents. The therapist can move the client into a light trance and do age regression work, in which the client relives some traumatic moments and the therapist champions the reversal of empathy in trance. One may use guided imagery, as I did with Ryan, or the power of a group, as was effective with George. There are any number of ways to redo the original inversion.

What they all have in common is the conviction that the deal men are offered by patriarchy is ultimately of no great benefit to them—even though it does afford them certain privileges.

In order to help men question and ultimately distance themselves from a host of accustomed but unfruitful behaviors I have found it useful to first understand the ways in which the man's particular abuse history, as well as forces in the culture at large, have set him up to be immature or unskilled in the realm of relationship (empathic holding). Then we look squarely together at the cost, to him and to those around him, should he continue in the same vein (confrontation). Faced with such a combination of understanding and clarity, I have found few men refuse to embark on an exploration of new repertoires of behavior, repertoires which, I am convinced, will leave them less depressed and less impoverished in the long run.

CONCLUSION

If the theme of disconnection is implicated in the transmission of injury, in toxic fathering, then reconnection, re-membering, is the cure. Refathering is a slow, sometimes painful relearning of *how to take care*–how to listen to and cherish those inner voices which have been stilled, how to listen to and cherish the needs of those around us. The great challenge for men of this generation, men who seem to be questioning the constraints of traditional roles, lies in understanding that in order to teach our sons how to move into adulthood with unrepudiated hearts, we must show them ours.

Fathering sons in this culture has too often been about depriving the child's deepest emotional needs while simultaneously pumping him up with false privilege. Real "fathering" by man or woman, by a therapist to a client, a father to a son, a man to a part of himself, is about holding the child at once with empathy and accountability. Fathering, as I see it, is about bringing the child into cherishing the skills of relational maturity, skills which include sensitivity to others (the traditional domain of women) and public assertive action (the traditional domain of men).

If each father is a bridge, stretching from the generation behind to the promise ahead, if each father transmits to his children—in parts knowingly, in parts not—the legacy of what it means to be a man, then each child, and particularly each son, offers the father an opportunity to transform that masculine legacy. To my mind this is the deepest sense of the idea that fatherhood is a crisis for each man. It is, above all, a crisis in identity with all of the difficulty and all of the transformative potential any real crisis affords. If he is to be authentic, a father's capacity to shape the legacy of masculinity he passes on to his children requires nothing less of him than a willingness to reshape the terms of masculinity by which he himself has lived. We men will be able to father our sons maturely to the degree to which we learn to father ourselves maturely.

AUTHOR NOTE

I am indebted to a number of people for their help, inspiration and support: above all to Olga Silverstein for lending me intellectual courage, to Jack Sternbach for lending me wit, to Pia Mellody for her wisdom, and to Kathy Weingarten for her patience and editorial guidance. I wish also to acknowledge my debt to friends and colleagues at The Family Institute of Cambridge and the many generative conversations with them over the years. Most of the thoughts contained in this article are elaborated further in a forthcoming book, *Breaking the Chain: Men, Masculinity and Depression*, Houghton Mifflin.

NOTES

1. I am indebted to the pioneering work of Joe Pleck (1983) for many of these thoughts.

2. See Pleck (1981, 1983) and Solomon (1982) for reviews of the literature.

3. I am particularly indebted to Olga Silverstein for helping me clarify my thinking on this point. Cf. Bergman (1991), Betcher & Pollack (1993), Silverstein (1994) and Weingarten (1994).

4. The principle here is an old one. Advocate for or too strongly identify with an oppressed group and risk a similar oppression–the fate of the "Indian lover," "Jew lover," "Nigger lover." The fate of the sissy. The film, "Casualties of War," dramatizes the true story of a young American soldier who stands against his peers in their capture and repeated rape of a Vietnamese woman. He is taunted, assaulted and finally threatened with rape himself.

5. Mellody (1989) uses the terms *overt* and *covert* abuse to mean both open versus secret as well as what I call here "active" versus "passive." See also Janoff-Bulman (1992) and McCann & Pearlman (1990) especially pp. 57-79.

6. See Mellody (1989) on the issue of "carried feelings."

REFERENCES

Bergman, S. (1991). Men's psychological development: A relational perspective. *Work in Progress, No. 48*. Wellesley, MA: Stone Center Working Paper Series.

Biller, H. (1974). *Fatherhood: A sociological perspective*. Lexington, MA: Heath.

Betcher, W. and Pollack, W. (1993). *In a time of fallen heroes: The recreation of masculinity*. New York: Athenaeum.

Bloch, J. (1978). Debatable conclusions about sex differences. *Contemporary Psychology, 2*, 517-522.

Bograd (1993). Women treating men. Paper presented at MAMFT, Springfield, MA.

Chodorow, N. (1978). *The reproduction of mothering*. Berkeley: University of California Press.

Connell, R.W. (1987). *Gender and power*. Stanford: Stanford University Press.

Crosby, F. (1991). *Juggling: The unexpected advantages of balancing career and home for women and their families*. New York: The Free Press.

Crowley, J.D. (1991). *Silencing the self: Depression and women*. Cambridge, Massachusetts: Harvard University Press.

Fein, R. (1977). Examining the nature of masculinity. In G. Sargent (ed.), *Beyond sex roles*. St. Paul: West.

Gelinas, D. (1988). The persisting negative effects of incest. *Psychiatry, 46*, 312-332.

Gough, H. (1952). Identifying psychological femininity. *Educational and Psychological Measurement, 12*, 427-439.

Hochshild, A. (1990). *The second shift*. New York: Viking Penguin.

Janoff-Bulman, R. (1992). *Shattered assumptions: Toward a new psychology of trauma.* New York: The Free Press.

Juster, F.T. (1987). A note on recent changes in time use. In F.T. Juster & F. Stafford (Eds.), *Studies in the measurement of time allocation.* Ann Arbor, MI: Institute for Social Research.

Levinson, D. (1978). *The season's of a man's life.* New York: Knopf.

Lamb, M. (ed.), (1986). *The father's role: Applied perspectives.* New York: Wiley & Sons.

Levant, R. (1992). Toward the reconstruction of masculinity, *Journal of Family Psychology,* 5, 379-402.

McCann, I.L. & Pearlman, L.A. (1990). *Psychological trauma and the adult survivor.* New York: Brunner/Mazel.

Mellody, P. (1989). *Facing codependence.* New York: Harper and Row.

Meth, R. & Pasick, R. (Eds.) (1990). *Men In therapy: The challenge of change.* New York: Guilford.

Miller, Jean Baker (1976). *Toward a new psychology of women.* Boston: Beacon Press.

Minuchin, S. (1974). *Families and family therapy.* Cambridge, MA: Harvard University Press.

Munsen & Rutherford (1963). Parent-child relations and parental personality in relation to young children's sex-role preferences. *Child Development,* 34, 589-607.

Osherson, S. (1986). *Finding our fathers.* New York: Fawcett Columbine.

Pleck, J. (1981). *The myth of masculinity.* Cambridge, Massachusetts: The MIT Press.

Pleck, J. (1983). Husbands' and wives' paid work and family roles: Current research issues. In H. Lopata & J. Pleck (Eds.), *Research in the interweave of social roles, families, and jobs.* Greenwich, CT: Jai Press.

Real, T. (1978). Projective-introjective cycles in marital interaction: A psychoanalytic/sociological inquiry. M.S.W. Thesis, Smith College School for Social Work, Northampton, MA.

Silverstein, O. (1994). *The courage to raise good men.* New York: Viking Penguin Press.

Sitze, G. (1986). The division of task responsibilities in U.S. households: Longitudinal adjustments to change. *Social Forces,* 3, 199-216.

Solomon, K. (1982). The Masculine Gender Role. In N. Levy & K. Solomon (Eds.), *Men in transition: Theory and therapy.* New York: Plenum Press.

Steinbeck, J. (1952). *East of Eden.* New York: Viking Press.

Sternbach, J. (1992). A man's studies approach to group treatment with all-male groups. *Men's Studies Review Special Issue: Men and Mental Health,* 9, 21.

Weingarten, K. (1994). *The mother's voice: Strengthening intimacy in families.* New York: Harcourt Brace.

Woititz, J. (1983). *Adult children of alcoholics.* Hollywood, Fla.: Heath Communications Inc.

Boys Will Be Men:
A Response to Terry Real's Paper

Virginia Goldner

The most painful part of reading Terry Real's meditation on masculinity was coming upon the description of Janie, who, when stonewalled in her attempts to connect with her husband and sons, "amiably withdraws." It was her *cheerful* compliance with their cool, dismissive, invisible (and thus, deniable) rejection that got to me. As the mother of a son, our only child, I am often coping with the feeling of being "on the outside." And I know well the strategy of giving up and drifting off without a fuss.

In our household, the family drama does not include the father's masculine devaluation of relatedness. Rather, this father and son share a dense and nuanced relationship: a world of activities, memories, jokes, and lore. They slip into a groove together, like the old friends they are, and I envy and resent their easy familiarity. I also feel bad about myself for not fighting harder for a place at the table.

But when I really think about it, I realize that staying connected to a son *is* a constant challenge for mothers in our culture, despite personal motivation and family support for it. In these brief remarks, I shall make this point by focussing on two of the psycho-

Virginia Goldner, PhD, is a senior faculty member of the Ackerman Institute, 149 East 78th Street, New York, NY 10021.

[Haworth co-indexing entry note]: "Boys Will Be Men: A Response to Terry Real's Paper." Goldner, Virginia. Co-published simultaneously in the *Journal of Feminist Family Therapy* (The Haworth Press, Inc.) Vol. 7, No. 1/2, 1995, pp. 45-48; and: *Cultural Resistance: Challenging Beliefs About Men, Women, and Therapy* (ed: Kathy Weingarten) The Haworth Press, Inc., 1995, pp. 45-48; and: *Cultural Resistance: Challenging Beliefs About Men, Women, and Therapy* (ed: Kathy Weingarten) Harrington Park Press, an imprint of The Haworth Press, Inc., 1995, pp. 45-48. *[Single or multiple copies of this article are available from The Haworth Document Delivery Service: 1-800-342-9678, 9:00 a.m. - 5:00 p.m. (EST).]*

© 1995 by The Haworth Press, Inc. All rights reserved.

45

cultural determinants of my "outside position." Both point to the way gender is created, performed and inscribed in our culture.

I don't agree with Terry Real that gender is an irrelevant vestigial category, although I completely support his impulse to dislodge and critique the arbitrary, dichotomizing distinctions that are made in its name. But gender is still the first, and probably the most decisive distinction that can be made about a person. Remember the research demonstrating that adults speak to and handle neonates totally differently, as a function of whether they are told the baby is a girl or a boy?

Given that we are born into a symbolic and material world that is *already* gendered in every possible way, it is impossible to overstate its effects on mind and culture. Gender is an identity category through which every detail of one's subjectivity is constituted, beginning before birth. We cannot "see through" gender to the person "inside," since gender and self have co-evolved throughout the developmental process. The paradox of gender is that while it is clearly not an essence that can be found in the core of the person, it still constitutes a core experience of identity, both psychological and social.

Moreover, culture is continually producing, in its incessant, multi-media fashion, new images and stories about what it means to be a man or woman now. All of us are swept up into these narratives, performing gender in compliance with, or in resistance to them. This means (to me) that we cannot simply substitute, as Terry Real proposes, the non-gendered category of "parenting" for the gender-saturated, ideologically charged categories of mothering and fathering, because our culture will continue to symbolize these practices in gendered terms. We can critique, disrupt, resist, and perhaps even transform maternal and paternal practice, but it will always "read" as male/female, *because it will always be enacted and observed by a gendered subject.*

Thus, I shall always be my son's *mother*, not simply his parent. And, because he is a male child, he and I will experience each other as fundamentally different, even if we are deeply bonded, and even if he has identified with me in many profound ways.

Which brings me back to the topic of my outside position in my own small family. In a variant on Terry Real's opening thought about how sons "remember what their fathers wish to forget," I believe that having children is one way we *all* rework, rethink, and repair our own experience of gender development and identity. When children are young, before gender and character fully claim and possess them, their porous androgyny allows us to "use" them as psychic containers for the imaginative repair of our own childhood hurts. But once they are conscripted by gender into one of its dichotomous entities, a door closes, and they are no longer all things to all people.

In fathering our son, my husband is always in some kind of dialogue with his own issues about masculinity. This continual working through of a central drama around gender "thickens" his experience of fathering in countless ways. While there are many meaningful and healing dimensions to my mothering of our boy, they do not include the reparative experience of getting another chance to work out the pains and pleasures of femininity. For that, I must look elsewhere (like writing this piece, for example, while my husband and son "shoot hoops" in the basketball net rigged up in our bedroom)!

Meanwhile, my son's agenda (which may change with his impending adolescence) has been very focussed on the project of turning himself into an All American Boy. This is because, I think, it was the only way he could find to fit into the world of his peers. He changed schools in first grade, moving from the warm, fuzzy androgynous context of his preschool to an academically rigorous, coed school which promoted gender divisions in ways that only became clear over time. A few months into the year, he began to talk about "feeling alone in school," which, sadly, turned out to be true.

As I observed him trying to make his way in the schoolyard, I began to notice that he was as "different" from the other boys as I was from their mothers. It was at that point that I realized that these 6-year-olds had *already been pushed out of the nest!* Not one could be found wrapped around a mother's leg or absent-mindedly crawling on a lap for a moment's refueling. Not one was wandering aimlessly about, lost in fantasy play. Instead, they were already organizing themselves into competitive sports! These little boys with no front teeth and no muscle tone were already performing the rites of masculinity that Terry Real has described: "to accept psychological neglect, to discount nurture and to turn the vice of such abandonment into a manly virtue."

We moved our son out of that school at the end of the academic year. He is now in the most culturally progressive, nurturant school in our city. But slowly, inexorably, he has stepped into the stream of male culture, nonetheless. My husband, for example, followed no sporting events until our son began to talk of nothing else. In one of the many paradoxes of gender conscription, our 12-year-old has recruited his father back into the world of scores and skill and power, a world where, if you don't win, you lose. And though our son is not a natural athlete, he has devoted himself to becoming passable at baseball and basketball. In fact, until a year ago, he was actually capable of imagining that if he worked at it, he could "get called up to the majors(!)"

These grandiose delusions are harmless, and probably necessary, since his athletic ability is fairly limited. In this mad, fantastical project of becoming "one of the boys," our son is learning things about practice and perserverance, about the pleasures of a strong and coordinated body, and about sportsmanship.

But team sports is not a world I know or care about, and I'd just as soon pass the ball to my husband who can repair the pain of having had a father who didn't notice, and didn't help him play sports during those years when everything depended on it.

Sometimes I think I should just settle for being the mom in the bleachers who carries the drinks, the sunblock and the memories of an earlier time when boys could nuzzle, play and rest in the maternal sphere. But the mood passes. As, for example, when my son got the idea that his surprise birthday present to me this year would be . . . "Him!" He gave me a hand-drawn card that promised to spend a day, just the two of us, doing what he thought I'd like to do. This included the incredible surprise of taking me ice-skating in Rockefeller Center, something I hadn't done since I was . . . *his* age!

Lesbian and Gay Parents:
From Margin to Center

Laura Benkov

SUMMARY. The increasing visibility and presence of families headed by lesbians and gay men poses critical challenges to dominant notions of family. Yet psychological research has for the most part missed this challenge by conceptualizing lesbian and gay headed families as marginal and comparing them in a normative way to the heterosexual, nuclear model. In this paper I propose instead a social constructionist, feminist approach to research and clinical practice–an approach that places lesbian and gay headed families at the center, rather than on the margins. This approach eschews a priori theories, breaks down the binary researcher/subject opposition, and focuses on multiple, sometimes conflicting, narrative strands. I argue that such an approach yields new perspectives on the nature of social change, the relationship between individuals and culture, and the meaning of family. *[Single or multiple copies of this article are available from The Haworth Document Delivery Service: 1-800-342-9678, 9:00 a.m. - 5:00 p.m. (EST).]*

In this paper I want to explore my journey toward creating a different kind of research from that which I have read before dealing with the lives of lesbian and gay parents. I argue for the advan-

Laura Benkov, PhD, is a Supervising Psychologist in the Department of Psychiatry, Children's Hospital, 2 Longwood Avenue, Boston, MA 02115.

[Haworth co-indexing entry note]: "Lesbian and Gay Parents: From Margin to Center." Benkov, Laura. Co-published simultaneously in the *Journal of Feminist Family Therapy* (The Haworth Press, Inc.) Vol. 7, No. 1/2, 1995, pp. 49-64; and: *Cultural Resistance: Challenging Beliefs About Men, Women, and Therapy* (ed: Kathy Weingarten) The Haworth Press, Inc., 1995, pp. 49-64; and: *Cultural Resistance: Challenging Beliefs About Men, Women, and Therapy* (ed: Kathy Weingarten) Harrington Park Press, an imprint of The Haworth Press, Inc., 1995, pp. 49-64. *[Single or multiple copies of this article are available from The Haworth Document Delivery Service: 1-800-342-9678, 9:00 a.m. - 5:00 p.m. (EST).]*

© 1995 by The Haworth Press, Inc. All rights reserved.

49

tages, perhaps even necessity, of using a feminist/social constructionist framework to understand lesbian and gay parenting. I am
going to use this forum to explore the connections between the way
I approach my research and what has emerged from that approach
thus far. I see these as intricately linked–it is no coincidence that
both my way of working, an amalgam of feminist, social constructionist and narrative frameworks, and the subject matter of my
work, lesbian and gay parents, fall outside the mainstream. I question not just the methods but also the underlying assumptions in
much of the existing psychological literature on lesbian and gay
parents. I want, simultaneously, to highlight a few of the many
fascinating possibilities for thinking and living that lesbian and gay
parents open up for all of us (Benkov, 1994).

PART I:
FINDING AN APPROACH TO RESEARCH

In this paper I will explore the consequences of shifting perspective–of moving lesbian and gay parents from the margin to the
center of thought. This shift has not been easy for me to accom-
plish–there is much that weighs against it. Homophobia and an
idealization of the traditional nuclear family pervade American
thinking. Psychology is no exception, and even where researchers
have tried to counter rather than perpetuate these two modes of
thought, they have still placed their work in relation to it. In trying
to disprove basically homophobic and heterosexist assumptions,
they have often made those assumptions the center of their studies.

I bring to my work a longstanding affinity with feminist and
social constructionist endeavors. Perhaps most influential on my
research have been the many feminist explorations of silence and
absence of particular voices. For instance, Adrienne Rich has written eloquently about the silence that surrounds lesbianism and
women's experiences. She says ". . . Silence can be a plan rigor-
ously executed–the blueprint to a life–It is a presence–it has a
history a form–Do not confuse it–with any kind of absence . . ."
(Rich, 1978). So, too, Carol Gilligan redirected inquiry in developmental psychology simply by pointing out how much theory that
was supposedly about human development had been based on

research that completely ignored girls' and women's perspectives (Gilligan, 1982).

Influenced by writers such as these in my early twenties, I grew up, as a thinker, acutely attuned to which voices were present and which were absent in all theory construction. Feminists have done the most to articulate the parameters and consequences of this dimension of knowledge. However, attention to absent voices also fits into a social constructionist view, one that, as Kenneth Gergen most succinctly summed up, postulates that "knowledge is not something people possess in their heads, but rather something people do together (Gergen, p. 270)." In a social constructionist framework, knowledge is not a matter of uncovering but rather of creating meaning. The process of meaning creation occurs in a social context and is intricately bound to power relations, with some voices having more weight and social legitimacy than others.

This work began from the most personal space imaginable. At nineteen I found myself in love with a woman, trying to reconcile my sense that I would live as a lesbian with the fact that I passionately wanted to be a mother. I knew no lesbian mothers and the only ones I'd heard of had had children in heterosexual marriages before coming out. What I remember most vividly about the early days of these "lesbian/mother" feelings and ideas is walking through Greenwich Village with my lover imagining we were the only two lesbians even contemplating such a scenario. It is an image I am struck by now, for surely, unbeknownst to us, on those streets we passed dozens of other such couples, and at least a few who were already lesbian mothers.

A few years later, having understood there were lesbians choosing motherhood (it was the early eighties, the first wave of the lesbian baby boom) but still finding myself in a very isolated conversation with my lover, I was standing in the hallway at my graduate school trembling, as I told my faculty advisor that I wanted to write my dissertation on lesbian mothers. I remember glancing over my shoulder–afraid someone would hear me, and then being moved to reflect on that fear. What was the point of the work, if not eventually to be heard?

From that whispered intention came a dissertation project–the first step of which was a literature review. Amidst the fluorescent lights and stacks upon stacks of psychology journals, I searched for images of myself and of the women I would soon interview, but of course found none. I was not naive, and hadn't really expected to find myself represented in these journals. Yet as I looked around the room and took in the sheer vastness of the quantity of writing in which I was nowhere to be found, it felt like that moment in a horror film, when one passes by a mirror and sees no reflection.

What I did find in the journals was that beginning in 1979 there were studies comparing lesbian headed families (subsequent to heterosexual divorce) with those of single heterosexual or married heterosexual mothers. The studies all addressed questions such as whether children were more prone to be lesbian or gay, to have "confused" sex role identities or behaviors, or to be otherwise "pathological." What emerged clearly in the course of examining this scant literature on lesbian mothers, is that the psychological studies were a direct outgrowth of the increasing number of lesbian mother custody cases appearing in court. The questions had been framed to respond to the issues arising in judicial settings–thus the link between social context and psychological research was very obvious in this instance. The studies did not describe families headed by lesbians in any rich detail–they did not give any indication of what life in these families was like. Instead they focussed on what was not true about lesbian headed families–what the children were not. That is to say, they were not more likely to be gay, to be confused about their gender roles or to be pathological.

Lesbian mothers had gone from total invisibility in the literature, that is from total absence, to a peculiar kind of presence–one that remained close to absence because it was fundamentally shaped and limited by heterosexist and homophobic assumptions.

The existent studies held, at their centers, a traditional nuclear family model and a model of heterosexuality as normative. Lesbian headed families were, from this perspective, on the margins to be compared normatively to heterosexual family structures. By normative I mean the comparison was not simply "like" and "unlike," but rather "like–normal" and "unlike–deviant."

Obviously, this way of thinking about lesbian mothers had made sense to many. In fact, it had been crucial to the outcomes in a multitude of lesbian mother custody trials. While appreciative of that fact, the studies (and more importantly their status as the only studies) distressed me greatly. From my perspective they stated the obvious, did not question homophobic assumptions, and rendered a flat picture, devoid of nuance and texture, of families headed by lesbians.

I was uncomfortable with the existing lesbian mother studies for many reasons. I don't see the traditional nuclear family as a normative model which should set standards for all others to meet. I don't think it matters whether children grow up to be lesbian or gay, or construct their sense of gender in non-traditional ways. In both these respects, the studies took up rather than questioned homophobic and heterosexist assumptions.

But there were even deeper levels at which these studies troubled me. I don't think that family structure is particularly relevant to the issue of optimal human development. I believe instead that children's present and future well-being depends on the quality of relationships in their world, not on the structure of their families. And I see these qualitative questions as important not only within whatever family structures children have, but equally so, in the rest of their environment–in communities and the larger society. Are children loved and cared for in their homes, are they in danger of being shot when they walk out their doors, do they attend schools that nurture their growth and build self-esteem, are they discriminated against or welcomed in the world, can they expect to have meaningful work, or even any work, when they grow up? In short are their worlds filled with possibilities and lessons of love or with stultification and lessons of hate?

There is another aspect to my discomfort with these studies that link family structure to the question of "pathology"–this one relating to the position of psychologists in society. I don't see any professionals, including psychologists, as the proper arbiters of what constitutes ideal human existence. In particular, I don't see the sorts of standardized measures used in empirical psychological research as adequate to capture much of what matters in human experience.

Though perhaps not readily apparent, this set of criticisms are interwoven. I am concerned about where my work fits into society as a whole. I see work such as the studies I'm critiquing as accepting a set of assumptions that are quite dangerous. When psychologists become the arbiters of what constitutes optimal human existence, and when, from that position, they do studies that assume a link between family structure and children's mental health or illness, their work is very much in line with the current vogue of reducing complex social problems to the question of family structure. When they find that "deviance" from the normative nuclear model does not in fact produce "pathology," they certainly push beyond some limits of the "family values" way of thinking. But they don't question its most basic assumptions.

I write this critique with much ambivalence for though I believe all I have just stated, I am also acutely aware of the enormous value of the studies I am questioning. Clearly, they made a difference in the lives of lesbian and gay parents, and they did so precisely because they were in line with both the form and content of mainstream thinking. That is to say, they were taken seriously in the judicial system precisely because the researchers embraced the role that society gives psychologists as arbiters of emotional health, they took seriously the assumed linkage between family structure and children's well-being, and they made central the concern about whether children raised by homosexuals would grow up to be gay.

I am aware, as I simultaneously critique these studies and appreciate what they accomplished, that I write from a particular historical vantage point. I have the luxury to look beyond such frameworks, because these studies already exist. Lesbian and gay parents still lose custody in court, but, in contrast to the early seventies, there is now a body of respected literature that can be brought to their defense.

Perhaps I am emblematic of the evolution of lesbian and gay voices as a currently popular gay rights slogan goes, "Homophobia? Get over it." As with all marginalized groups, the progress of lesbians and gay men depends in part on being able to answer to and dismantle stereotypes, but that is a process that becomes, rather quickly, quite tiresome. It's unacceptable to be limited to constantly defining oneself in contrast to myths. I was fortunate in beginning my work from a position of both wanting to move beyond such limits and of having the opportunity to do so.

The center of my work was not heterosexual norms or societal givens, but rather the lesbian mothers, gay fathers, and children I spoke with. It was their diversity as much as their commonality that intrigued me. As I moved more deeply into the conversations with lesbian and gay parents, one question continued to plague me. Was there room in the world for this work–for their voices and mine? I decided to speak into the void and find out.

If I was not going to conduct an empirical study replete with control groups and measures of "pathology," what was I going to do? A favorite artist of mine–Alan Magee, a realist painter–describes his work in much the way I conceive of mine. One could substitute research or psychology for "art" in the following quote. "I believe that art should work to reacquaint us with the shared details of our lives. We need often to be reminded of the details. We need to know them, not as props in a false and nostalgic narrative but as vital autonomous characters in the irreducibly interrelated universe that we share with them . . . (Magee, 1987)." As Magee goes on to say, this seemingly ordinary goal turns out in practice to be extraordinary–both rare and of significant consequence. He says "It is difficult to keep ourselves attentive to these skins and faces. They inconvenience us. But they are needed, for they bring us back from our absence, our abstractedness (Magee, 1987)." In taking on such an endeavor, the process is as important as the outcome. Magee describes his process of drawing as a kind of attending during which he comes to "regard my subjects differently–anything that I have observed carefully seems to spring free from its assigned category, and begins to speak through its individual and specific nature" (Magee, 1987).

In framing my own work this way over the years, I have felt myself to be swimming against the tide of professional psychology. That is to say, I have found many categories of psychological theory and standard research approaches to do the opposite of Magee's "art"–to render us more abstracted and absent rather than present to the world we live in, and I have therefore ventured out in search of other ways of looking.

As I've tried to translate Magee's painterly attention to "skins and faces" into the realm of social science research, three key elements have emerged as central to my own process. They concern my relationship to my subjects, the kind of listening stance I strive for, and the focal points of my inquiry.

1. My Relationship to My Subjects

I use the word subject here in a dual sense of "the subject matter," and the people I interviewed. For all that psychologists often choose research topics that are close to home, I think there is a strong pull toward approaching even those issues chosen for very personal reasons from a distant, objectifying (supposedly objective) stance.

I have always been distressed by the fact that as clinicians we tend to write about therapy primarily from our positions and experiences as therapists, with clients framed in the writing as "other" despite the fact that most of us have certainly been clients, and hopefully have learned as much about doing therapy from that position as from our professional practices. Yet we rarely write in professional journals about those insights.

Similarly, I think psychologists generally position themselves as researchers with subjects as "other," and I think there is a great deal lost through this rigid positioning. In both clinical and research literature, clients or subjects can be spoken about in such a way that readers most certainly disidentify with them–that is to say, they are so objectified that to identify with them is to feel acute alienation.

I explicitly eschew such a rigid researcher/subject split in my work, viewing myself as simultaneously both subject and researcher in myriad ways. My desire to do the work in the first place grew out of my sense of invisibility as well as my simple need to know more about lesbian parenthood, a phenomenon that would be a critical part of my own life. This shaped not only the questions I asked, but also my relationships with the people I interviewed, many of whom took an older sibling advising kind of role with me or saw me as a vehicle through which their stories could be given voice (made visible and made to count). My relation to my subjects was like that of a young person to elders in a tribe–essentially all of these people had something vital to teach me.

Despite my identification with my subjects I never saw myself as the same as any of them (or any of them as the same as each other for that matter). In this work, what I value most is the combination of empathic identification and acute respect for and interest in difference.

2. Listening Stance

Throughout my work I believed that the critical issues would reveal themselves to me. I made an effort not to impose an *a priori* frame, an effort I see as linked to feminist and social constructionist positions. This is obviously not to deny that I have a framework, a subjectivity, but it is to emphasize a certain kind of listening stance that has allowed subjects to take me places I did not imagine ahead of time, and to distinguish themselves from each other in my thinking.

3. The Focal Points of Inquiry

I did not, as a psychodynamic thinker might, focus exclusively on individual "intrapsychic" phenomenon, but rather saw social context as pivotal–that is the legal structures, adoption, and reproductive technology practices, were just as important focal points as the descriptions of lesbian and gay parents' lives. The subject matter of my research was not lesbian and gay parents per se but rather the cultural phenomenon of lesbian and gay parenting. This meant I looked primarily at the meanings people create with each other, particularly around the phenomenon of family.

In doing so I focussed not on singular coherent narrative strands, but rather on narratives as incorporating multiple layers and voices. This focus often renders the junctures, or meeting points of social layers or conflicting voices, as the most interesting places to look. Disjunctures in language use within families as well as conflicts between the state's definition of family and families' self-definitions became primary focal points of my work.

For instance, in one family the different uses of language may mean that a child considers she has two mothers while her grandmother considers she has only one. How does such an early experience of differing definitions of "mother" affect consciousness? Furthermore, the state, like the grandmother in this instance, defines "family" as including one, not two, mothers–a move which often has devastating consequences for children whose lesbian parents split up or whose biological or legal adoptive parent dies.

Yet the relationship between culture and individuals is not uni-directional. While lesbians and gay men creating new family forms are affected by the traditional notions of "family" embedded in their surrounding communities and social institutions such as the legal system, they also challenge these notions to change. Some grand-mothers learn that their grandchildren do indeed have two mothers and, as of this writing, some states legally recognize two-mother and two-father families through "second-parent adoptions."

PART II:
A QUESTION EMERGES:
WHAT IS A FAMILY?

Listening to the stories of lesbian and gay parents lives without imposing an *a priori* frame, attending to the multiple strands of their narratives, and recognizing my own struggles as part of the phe-nomenon I was studying, my research began to take form. One question cropped up over and over again. It was a question that startled me with its simultaneous complexity and simplicity. What had happened was much like Magee's description of his painting process. Something had moved from being a prop in a "false and nostalgic narrative" to being a "vital autonomous character in the irreducibly interrelated universe" (Magee, 1987). That something was Family itself. I found myself asking with an urgency that sur-prised me, "What indeed is a family?" That of course was the question that the lesbian and gay parents I spoke with were grap-pling with on a daily basis. And it was the question they were challenging all of us to face.

By following lesbian and gay parents into this territory where the creation of family is in process, I came to see my subjects not as families on the margin to be compared to a central norm, but rather, as people on the cutting edge of a key social shift, from whom there was much to be learned about the meaning of family and about the nature of social change.

It is impossible in this space to convey all the levels on which this learning took place, so to illustrate my point I will focus on the question of what defines parenthood when lesbian or gay couples jointly raise children. In families where children were conceived or adopted in a previous heterosexual relationship and in those where a couple chose to have children together, there is a question as to whether both couple members are parents, and more specifically, whether both are mothers or fathers. Families answer this question in many different ways and the answers in any given family arise from multiple levels of experience. In fact there may be conflict about this issue within an individual's mind, within a couple, between a couple and their extended family, or between a family and the larger society.

The cultural consensus, which becomes part of many families' realities, is that children can't have two mothers or two fathers. There is little possibility of the state recognizing both couple members as parents–just as they cannot marry, for the most part as of now, lesbians and gay men can't adopt their partners' children. No matter how deeply and seriously one parents a child–that is relates with the kind of love and responsibility we associate with parenthood–it is often far more difficult for a lesbian or gay man to move beyond the role of parent's partner and establish a parental role of his or her own than, for example, it is for heterosexual stepparents.

This question of who gets to be a mother or father takes on even more complex dimensions in the context of lesbians and gay men choosing to raise children after coming out. These couples have the opportunity to construct their families together from the ground up.

When some lesbian or gay couples choose to have children, they may agree that one partner will not have a parental role. In these instances, not being a heterosexual couple procreating together allows room for a different kind of family definition. For couples where one person wishes to be a parent and the other doesn't, being lesbian or gay may function to provide the freedom to choose to define the family in a somewhat unusual way–that is with one parent and one adult who lives with and relates to the child, but not in a parental way.

However, while there are some for whom this type of arrangement is preferable, there are many lesbian and gay couples who want to define their families as two mothers or two fathers sharing the parenting of their children. Some are able to achieve this goal with little difficulty. Carol and May, for instance, are jointly raising two children that Carol conceived with a gay male friend, Richard.

Richard and his partner are involved with the children as secondary parents, visiting on weekends and joining in family gatherings. May stayed home with both children when they were young and took on a primary parenting role during that time. For May and Carol, the fact that Carol gave birth to the children is insignificant—both see themselves as mothers and are recognized by their extended families and community as such. They fully embrace the idea that mothering is a question of relationship, not biology.

Yet many lesbian couples I spoke with didn't have such an easy time creating family relationships like Carol and May's, though they wanted to. While many of these women spoke of mothering as a socially rather than biologically determined relationship this belied their actual family dynamics. In constructing their families they ended up matching primary parenting roles to biology. In contrast with their idea that mothering is primarily a socially rather than biologically determined role, women in these couples often expressed a different belief—their sense that the biological connection between mothers and children is powerfully defining of relationship whether one wants it to be or not.

Many couples think about these questions of symmetry and asymmetry ahead of time and structure their families to include some balance, for example deciding that each woman will bear a child. Some couples choose to adopt in order to avoid the asymmetry they see as inevitably stemming from biological connections. Yet, adoption can stand in for biology in some couples' minds. Since they cannot marry, by and large lesbians and gay men cannot adopt as couples, but must instead do single parent adoptions. The state therefore only recognizes one parent legally, just as in the case of biological conception. The fact that only one couple member has legal parent status may create a power imbalance that lurks beneath family dynamics subtly exerting influence.

Often the issue of who is a "real" parent is a matter not just of what the couple decides but of their relations to their extended families and communities. For instance two-year-old Roger's biological grandmother came to visit one week and in that short time changed the way he referred to his non-biological mother, Denise. Roger had gotten into the habit of calling her "Mommy," but his grandmother was appalled by this. She felt that Roger had one mother, not two, and she let him know by correcting him each time he called Denise "Mommy." Denise and Sharon were very upset but as they talked it over they decided to go along with the grand-mother's approach, although it saddened them to do so. Ultimately they saw grandmother's response as indicative of what others would do, and they worried about Roger having to deal with homo-phobia in the community. They felt he'd be safer if he had a more traditional way of naming his family. Denise and Sharon highlight how deeply homophobia may infiltrate family life.

Many lesbian and gay parents have an opposite response to homophobia or ignorance in the surrounding environment. They see it as their responsibilities to advocate for their children, to educate others about the truth of their family structure and to resist definitions that conflict with their own. One family for instance took great pains to correct people in the neighborhood who asked their daughter how her mommy was, requesting instead that they inquire about how her mommies were.

The question of who is a "real" or not "real" parent is even more interesting when one adds gender to the stew. For the most part, lesbians I spoke with were more likely to feel competitive around establishing two mother roles, while in contrast gay men talked little about difficulty establishing themselves as two fathers. The biological parameters of mothering and fathering contribute to this difference, with pregnancy, childbirth and nursing often setting up powerful dynamics for lesbians to contend with, which gay men don't face. But perhaps more significantly, this gender difference corresponds to the different socialization of men and women toward parenting. Women both expect of themselves and are expected by others to be primary parents, while the expectation for men is of a more secondary role. It is often therefore more difficult for a woman to feel like a "real" mother when she shares that role with someone who is clearly established and recognized in that position.

Conversely, some male couples I spoke with expressed more difficulty around sharing parenting labor and experienced more conflict about compromised work identities that resulted from devoting so much energy to the home. Craig and Jim, for example, had much conflict during the first year of their son's life because Jim, who ended up staying home more than Craig, felt both resentful and badly about himself. They hit a crisis point which resulted in working out what felt like a more equitable arrangement, but they also both realized that part of what needed to happen was a reassessment of their views of manhood.

While these aspects of lesbian and gay parenting fit gender stereotypes, in both instances lesbian and gay couples have to push themselves beyond traditional socialization. Women find themselves giving up the idea of being singularly primary parents and instead making room for another mother. Men who take on primary parenting responsibilities without wives to fall back on integrate this shift of priorities into their lives and identities, developing new models of masculinity.

CONCLUSION:
RESEARCH AND CLINICAL PRACTICE
IN A CHANGING SOCIAL CONTEXT

Families headed by lesbians and gay men certainly highlight how deeply embedded in society families really are–how much a matter of socially created meaning each family unit is. But they also show us the converse–that is, how individuals, in creating new ways of being together, influence the larger society. On the issue for instance of who is a "real" parent, questions are now arising in courts as lesbian and gay parents split up. Whereas ten years ago there was little legal discourse on what constitutes parenthood, now it is the subject of heated debate. For the most part the state continues to rely on biology and heterosexual marriage as determinative of parental status. In most lesbian and gay splits the non-biological parent has not even been given the right to a hearing about custody or visitation, being as one court put it, a "biological stranger." But some recent decisions go against this tide, and many more express the sentiment, even when they haven't decided on these grounds, that what should determine parent status is not biology or legal convention, but rather, the quality of relationship. In the emergence of this legal discourse, one can see how profoundly lesbian and gay parents open up the question of what really matters, what really counts as family, and of how we as a society are going to construct families.

The meaning of family is changing, and lesbian and gay parents are on the frontiers of that change. When one stops looking at them as on the margins, to be compared with the traditional nuclear model, new worlds open up. Lesbian and gay parents have much to teach the culture as a whole about different possibilities for intimacy, about creating change, and about the reciprocal relationship between individuals and society.

Ultimately the deeper I have gotten into this research the more the category of family expands–as it becomes a more inclusive category, it also becomes more centered on relational issues such as love and commitment. At the same time, the institution of family as deeply embedded in a heterosexual nuclear family normative model is highlighted through this work. The power of family as an institution–one replete with particular gendered roles, constructs of biology and heterosexuality–that is to say with ideological as well as concrete legal aspects–is revealed. Lesbian and gay parents challenge the institution even as they form their families in its shadow.

The research approach I propose here is particularly well suited to study such changing social phenomena insofar as it highlights disjunctures between dominant and marginal discourses and places the researcher in an open, receptive stance, ready to appreciate hitherto unimagined realities. Similarly, this approach can be the basis for clinical work that yields new possibilities for both clinicians and clients. It entails abandoning *a priori* theories in favor of opening oneself to clients' descriptions, listening closely to multiple narrative strands and the disjunctures between them, and attending carefully to the complex, reciprocal relationship between clients and all parts of their social contexts. Working this way as clinicians and researchers, we can create a psychology that, in Magee's words, helps us to recognize the details of life "not as props in a false and nostalgic narrative but as vital autonomous characters in the irreducibly interrelated universe that we share with them."

REFERENCES

Benkov, L. (1994). *Reinventing the family*. New York: Crown Publishers.
Gergen, K. (1985). The social constructionist movement in modern psychology. *American Psychologist*, 40 (3), 266-275.
Gilligan, C. (1982). *In a different voice: Psychological theory and women's development*. Cambridge: Harvard University Press.

Golombok, S., Spencer, A., Rutter, M. (1983). Children in lesbian and single-parent households: *Psychosexual and Psychiatric Appraisal. Child Psychology and Psychiatry*, 24 (4), 551-572.

Hill, M. (1987). Child-rearing attitudes of black lesbian mothers. In Lesbian Psychologies, Ed. *The Boston lesbian psychologies collective*, Illinois: University of Illinois Press, 215-227.

Hoeffer, B. (1981, July). Children's acquisition of sex-role behavior in lesbian-mother families. *American Journal of Orthopsychiatry*, 51 (3), 536-544.

Kirkpatrick, M., Smith, C., Roy, R. (1981, July). Lesbian mothers and their children: A comparative survey. *American Journal of Orthopsychiatry*, 51 (3), 545-551.

Lewin, E. (1981, Spring). Lesbianism and motherhood: Implications for child custody. *Human Organization*, 40, 6-13.

Magee, A. (1987). *Stones and other works*. New York: Harry N. Abrams, Inc.

Miller, J., Jacobsen, B., Bigner, J. (1981, Fall). The child's home environment for lesbian vs. heterosexual mothers: A neglected area of research. *Journal of Homosexuality*, 7 (1), 49-56.

Patterson, C. (1992, October). Children of lesbian and gay parents. *Child Development*, 63 (5), 1025-1042.

Rand, C., Graham, D., Rawlings, E. (1982). Psychological health and factors the court seeks to control in lesbian mother custody trials. *Journal of Homosexuality*, 8 (1), 27-39.

Rich, A. (1978). The dream of a common language. New York: W.W. Norton and Company.

Response to Laura Benkov, "Lesbian and Gay Parents: From Margin to Center"

Joan Laird

Lesbian and gay studies are very gradually entering the postmodern era. Like most work in the social science and mental health literature, research on lesbian and gay individuals, couples, and families has been dominated by positivist, objectivist thought. As valuable as the post-Stonewall research effort has been in some ways, as Laura Benkov points out, in other ways the everyday lives–the "cultures"–of lesbians, gays, and their families have remained invisible. The psychological metaphor has dominated lesbian and gay research, meaning that lesbians and gays have been measured on virtually every mental health and social adaptation scale available, a deficit-based effort that has surfaced few differences between gays and everyone else and has obscured rich, within-group diversity (Laird, 1993). Benkov, leaning on social constructionist and feminist thought, seeks to find a new path to more meaningful understanding of this marginalized, often invisible, group.

Borrowing a metaphor from African-American scholar bell hooks, she seeks to move lesbian and gay families "from margin to

Joan Laird, MS, LICSW, is Professor of Social Work at the Smith College School for Social Work, Northampton, MA 01063.

[Haworth co-indexing entry note]: "Response to Laura Benkov, Lesbian and Gay Parents: From Margin to Center." Laird, Joan. Co-published simultaneously in the *Journal of Feminist Family Therapy* (The Haworth Press, Inc.) Vol. 7, No. 1/2, 1995, pp. 65-67; and: *Cultural Resistance: Challenging Beliefs About Men, Women, and Therapy* (ed: Kathy Weingarten) The Haworth Press, Inc., 1995, pp. 65-67; and: *Cultural Resistance: Challenging Beliefs About Men, Women, and Therapy* (ed: Kathy Weingarten) Harrington Park Press, an imprint of The Haworth Press, Inc., 1995, pp. 65-67. *[Single or multiple copies of this article are available from The Haworth Document Delivery Service: 1-800-342-9678, 9:00 a.m. - 5:00 p.m. (EST).]*

© 1995 by The Haworth Press, Inc. All rights reserved.

center," to the middle rather than the periphery of her narrative lens. This article is a *bricolage,* a collection of fragments of ideas that are more deeply developed in the larger work based on her interviews with lesbian and gay parents (Benkov, 1994). In like fashion, I will reflect on just a few of the many provocative notions she sprinkles throughout the text.

First, the author's "I" voice is most refreshing. Reflecting a trend in postmodern writing, Benkov the researcher screens herself into rather than out of her work and her writing. This approach, which renders research a co-evolutionary experience, which recognizes that the student is part of the studied and that one's own experiences and meanings are relevant, was once scoffed at. Margaret Mead, for example, whose own familial and cultural experiences provided grist for her anthropological mill, like many female scholars was ridiculed for her "unscientific" work. Today James Clifford and George Marcus (1986), who devalue the importance of feminist research, have been credited with helping to revolutionize modern anthropological thought with their (heavily feminist but unacknowledged) notion that culture is "written" by the researcher.

Speaking of anthropology, the second point I wish to make is that Benkov's approach to research draws heavily on anthropological tradition and particularly on contemporary ethnographic method, although she does not make that linkage explicit here. She indicates that she draws upon social constructionist, feminist, and narrative ideas, focusing on "multiple, conflicting, narrative strands." Like Anderson and Goolishian (1992), she begins with a "not-knowing" stance, bracketing *a priori* theories in an effort to be fully open to listening closely to the stories of her informants, to the commonalities and differences and to the intricate relationships between them and the social contexts in which their daily lives are embedded. Although it is not clear from this brief piece what approach she will take in weaving those multiple threads together, her approach to the research itself promises to move toward what is badly needed in lesbian and gay studies–"thick description"–that is, richly detailed narratives of everyday life, narratives that will unpack the intricate experiences and meanings of the lesbian and gay family world "from the native's point of view."

Benkov, a psychologist, is less interested in the psychology than in the culture of lesbian and gay life. She wants to know how lesbian and gay families construct themselves and how, in so doing, they, in turn, create the world, pioneering new ways of being in family. Here we get just a tantalizing taste of that process, as she deftly illustrates how "disjunctures" in language use between lesbians and gays and the world around them reflexively influence each other, shaping multiple layers of narrative. This is particularly so in the very process of defining "family," as meanings of family through the lens of the lesbian couple and those of the State clash, sometimes forcing both to change. Here is one of the places her work takes, in my view, an exciting and leading edge. For it is through language, the storying process, that the family creates and recreates itself. This process is particularly important to understand in the case of the lesbian and gay family, since family members have few cultural mirrors in which they are reflected and must, in a sense, create their families from both old and new fragments of glass.

In her larger work, Benkov explores how lesbian and gay families make use of intergenerational family culture, heterosexual or not, how they blend the tried and the true with the innovative and unknown. Older and successful ways of being in family, of coupling, parenting, and dealing with the world, are not "owned" by heterosexuals. The making of a lesbian family involves more than a process of "add egalitarian and stir." It involves a creative approach to the re-examination of how these families use both wider cultural materials and family traditions—of custom, ritual, narrative, folklore, mythology, roles, and so on—of all the things that constitute "family."

A postmodern approach to writing lesbian and gay lives means allowing their own stories, their own myth-making processes, to surface. Benkov's work contributes much to that effort.

REFERENCES

Benkov, L. (1994). *Reinventing the family.* New York: Crown Publishers.

Clifford, J., & Marcus, G. (1986). *Writing culture: The poetics and politics of ethnography.* Berkeley: University of California Press.

Laird, J. (1993). Lesbian and gay families. In F. Walsh (Ed.), *Normal family processes,* (Second edition), pp. 282-328. New York: Guilford.

A Narrative Approach
to So-Called Anorexia/Bulimia

David Epston
Fran Morris
Rick Maisel

SUMMARY. In this paper we detail steps in the process of getting free of anorexia/bulimia. An edited version of a correspondence between the first two authors follows that records Ms. Morris' experience in breaking free of a twenty-three year tyrannical relationship with anorexia/bulimia. The correspondence illustrates practices that assist persons in forging a new relationship with anorexia/bulimia. Finally, Ms. Morris evaluates the benefits of these practices. *[Single or multiple copies of this article are available from The Haworth Document Delivery Service: 1-800-342-9678, 9:00 a.m. - 5:00 p.m. (EST).]*

David Epston is Co-Director, The Family Centre, 6 Goring Road, Sandringham 4, Auckland, New Zealand. He would like to acknowledge Kathy Weingarten for the considerable editing that was required and the integrity to the spirit of the work with which she undertook it.

Fran Morris, c/o Solar Hill, 61 Western Avenue, Brattleboro, VT 05301.

Rick Maisel, PhD, is in private practice at the Redwood Centre, 2428 Dwight Way, Berkeley, CA 94704; and is an adjunct faculty member at the California School of Professional Psychology-Alameda, CA; and at John F. Kennedy University, Orinda, CA. He was responsible for the first draft of the non-correspondence part of this paper, drawing in part on the doctoral dissertation of Christie Platt, PhD (1992).

[Haworth co-indexing entry note]: "A Narrative Approach to So-Called Anorexia/Bulimia." Epston, David, Fran Morris, and Rick Maisel. Co-published simultaneously in the *Journal of Feminist Family Therapy* (The Haworth Press, Inc.) Vol. 7, No. 1/2, 1995, pp. 69-96; and: *Cultural Resistance: Challenging Beliefs About Men, Women, and Therapy* (ed: Kathy Weingarten) The Haworth Press, Inc., 1995, pp. 69-96; and: *Cultural Resistance: Challenging Beliefs About Men, Women, and Therapy* (ed: Kathy Weingarten) Harrington Park Press, an imprint of The Haworth Press, Inc., 1995, pp. 69-96. *[Single or multiple copies of this article are available from The Haworth Document Delivery Service: 1-800-342-9678, 9:00 a.m. - 5:00 p.m. (EST).]*

© 1995 by The Haworth Press, Inc. All rights reserved.

69

This paper is written in the memory of Ellen West:

> "I don't understand myself at all. It is terrible not to understand yourself. *I confront myself as a strange person.* I am afraid of myself; I am afraid of the feelings to which I am defenselessly delivered over every minute. This is the horrible part of my life: it is filled with dread. Existence is only torture. . . . Life has become a prison camp. . . . I long to be violated . . . and *indeed I do violence to myself every hour.*" (Binswanger, L., The Case of Ellen West. In May, R. et al., 1958, 254, 258, 255, emphasis added by Binswanger)

I (D.E.) have been using a narrative perspective in my work for the past eight years. This framework derives from a collaboration with Michael White. The practices I will be presenting in this paper have emerged over time through our working, talking, and teaching together (Epston, 1989; Epston et al., 1992; Epston and White, 1992; White, 1989; White and Epston, 1990). Since 1986, I have become passionately committed to better understand and assist those persons oppressed by so-called anorexia/bulimia. What prompted me, amongst other concerns, was my dawning realization of the ways by which the objectifying practices of weighing, assessing, and measuring of women associated with the discourses of psychology and psychiatry could very well co-produce what is referred to as anorexia/bulimia in those very persons oppressed by anorexia/bulimia (Tavris, 1992).

In October, 1986, Svetlana Ripon wrote me a letter which incited my concern. Her letter became one of the first inquiries on which the Anti-Anorexia/Bulimia League collaborated. It led to a day-long workshop entitled "The Co-Production of Anorexia/Bulimia versus The Co-Production of Anti-Anorexia/Bulimia."[1] The presenters were seven members of The Anti-Anorexia/Bulimia League, aged 16-51. I was one of them. I continue to serve in the capacity of archivist/anthologist of The League. This League is not a support group in the conventional sense of the word. It invented itself as an underground resistance movement. Tomm (1992) referred to The League as "a community of counter-practice."

STEPS IN THE PROCESS OF GETTING FREE
OF ANOREXIA/BULIMIA

The first step in getting free from anorexia/bulimia typically begins when a person becomes more fully aware of the physical, emotional, spiritual, and relationship costs of an allegiance to an anorexic/bulimic lifestyle. This "disenchantment" has often been foreshadowed by a feeling of losing control over, or being controlled further, by anorexia/bulimia. These persons have come to realize that the proverbial tail is now wagging the dog and that anorexia/bulimia has usurped their lives and occupied their minds. People often report that their lives have become almost unendurable. At this juncture, people feel required to choose between self-execution (through starvation to death or by other means) or a commitment to the repudiation of, and the opposition to, anorexia/bulimia. Several anti-anorexic/bulimic practices support their efforts to break the spell of anorexia/bulimia.

BREAKING THE SPELL OF ANOREXIA/BULIMIA

1. Engage Person(s) in an Externalizing Conversation About Anorexia/Bulimia

By speaking about anorexia/bulimia as something separate from and external to persons, linguistic space is opened for persons to engage in their own assessment and evaluation of anorexia's "rules of the concentration camp," its "voice,"[2] and the practices of self and relationship it requires, e.g., exile and isolation, self-surveillance, self-hatred, self-punishment/torture/execution, etc. Externalizing anorexia/bulimia also undermines guilt and self-blame and replaces them with "anorexia-blame." It challenges totalizing descriptions of the person as anorexic/bulimic. It provides a landscape in which to identify current or historical acts of resistance to the dictates of anorexia/bulimia and, thereby, recognize the real possibility of furthering that opposition in the present and future (Allen, 1993; Epston, 1993; Madigan, 1992; Tomm, 1989; White, 1984; White and Epston, 1990).

Julie, aged 30, commented in a recent meeting (7/15/93):

> If I hadn't objectified anorexia(bulimia), I'd feel scared and
> I'd soon be binging. I'd have no choice. The most I could ever
> have done in my life is what they told me at the hospital. It was
> to phone someone up for them to rescue me. But I'd say to
> them at the hospital: "I don't want to phone anyone; I want to
> eat and be sick." They would say: "You just have to try
> harder!" I'd say in reply, "If I could phone someone up, I
> wouldn't be in the situation I'm in." They were conflating my
> identity with the voice of anorexia and giving it (the voice of
> anorexia) a platform in therapy to speak itself. If speech is like
> an act and I was isolated, I would go into those hospital offices
> and speak "anorexia" for an hour and would not have put
> myself forward in speech anywhere else in that week. That
> happened for years . . .
>   Now when I recognize the voice, saying things like
> "You've left it so late in life to get your act together . . . you
> might as well give up because you are so old now . . . there's
> just no point . . . you are never going to find anyone to love . . ."
> instead of just feeling victimized by it, believing that IT is me,
> I think: "That's anorexia!" If I can get through this five min-
> utes of it trying to tear me down, I will be all right, even
> though the voice of anorexia is compelling and horrible. I have
> this unshakeable faith that it is really not that powerful. It is
> anorexia thinking . . . that's all.

2. Provide Ready Access to the Archives
of The Anti-Anorexia/Bulimia League

Initially, persons in the thrall of anorexia/bulimia will have difficulty recognizing the destructive and lethal practices of self and
relationship that anorexia/bulimia demands of them, even after pro-
longed or repeated hospitalizations and tube feedings. These persons are offered ready access to the archives of The League. They
are invited to hear and/or read anorexic/bulimic accounts and how
such persons "unmasked" anorexia's purposes/intentions, betrayals
and lies. The significance of the archival material cannot be over-

stated. These "readings" replace the well-known pathologizing practices of assessment interviews.

Excerpted from an interview with Rhonda, aged 19 (5/8/90):

> D: You were just reflecting on Sarah's comments about how when I asked her some sort of diagnostic, assessment-type questions, she immediately said: "I'm shrinking inside." You have some comments about that?
>
> R: Absolutely typical feeling. I've been to eight other therapists before and the questions they ask, they put you . . . I feel like I fly back in the chair, into the corner and just sort of sit there and tense up. It's horrible!

Unlike conventional pathologizing stories regarding persons' lives, these conversations, stories, that are in the archive are plotted around "liberation," "resistance," and "oppression." These stories, which can be conveyed through writing, or stored on audiotape or videotape, begin to provide an alternative vocabulary which is a prerequisite for any sense of oppression and any notion of resistance. These stories make available some hope for an anti-anorexic/bulimic future. As Julie has said, "In a way, the first time I, self-consciously, took the side of outrage, or perhaps self-consciously did anything at all, was when I listened to the tapes and in some way anorexia was exposed."

3. Offer Metaphorical Descriptions of the "Regime" of Anorexia/Bulimia

Metaphorical descriptions, (e.g., "the concentration camp of anorexia/bulimia," "living death," "being on death row," etc.) can help persons "unmask" or see through the ways anorexia/bulimia operates on people's lives, inviting associations which can enliven and enrich these descriptions. Persons can be invited to assess the extent to which such descriptions match or capture their experience of anorexia/bulimia in their lives. Persons are encouraged to invent metaphorical descriptions of their own. A high value is placed on the production of anti-anorexic/bulimic discursive practices and any novelties are hastily added to the anti-anorexic lexicon. In an anti-anorexic/bulimic therapy, persons are not a product of language but instead produce what W. Halliday refers to as an "anti-language," the primary purpose of which is to subvert medical and lay discourses on anorexia with a new vocabulary, and new language forms (Halliday, 1978). Language is politicized. The stripped down language of objectivity which holds these persons prisoner in an anorexia "talk," a talk that minimizes, restrains, restricts, undermines, and diminishes, is replaced by the "play" of a lush, extravagant and polysemic language. The "play" involves the unpacking of the implications of the metaphors on their experience of anorexia/bulimia in their lives in particular, and women's lives in general.

4. Encourage the Personification of Anorexia/Bulimia

Personifying anorexia/bulimia allows for the attribution of intentions (for example, "Does anorexia intend to have you sign your own death warrant?"), beliefs (for example, "Does anorexia believe you are worthless?"), or practices (for example, "Has he turned you against yourself by talking you into self-blame and self-torture?").

The following questions were directed to Bridget, aged 15, in the company of her older cousin and her partner, in order to personify anorexia/bulimia. Just prior to the meeting, Bridget and her caretakers had been warned by her medical advisor that she could very likely perish at any moment.

> D: I think you have to understand its motives, its purposes. Why do you think it would do this, would hurt people and make them think they were happy to die with an anorexic smile on their face? What lethal practices does it use to confound you, to confuse you? Now you're on death row, but somehow anorexia's keeping it from you, and the more it keeps it from you, the more likely it will kill you.
>
> B: Well, I feel physically fine.
>
> D: How does it do that? How do you think it confuses you? How do you think it tells you you're feeling fine when you're on the point of death? . . . Most people, when they are near death know they're being murdered or dying, right? How's anorexia doing this to you? . . . Why does it say to you that you are feeling good? Why does it do this? Why does it want to murder you? Why doesn't it want you to

protest? Why doesn't it want you to put up any resistance? Why does it want you to go to your death like a sheep?

TURNING AGAINST ANOREXIA/BULIMIA

5. Identify the Cognitive, Affective, Interpersonal and Behavioral Components of Anorexia/Bulimia

Once the person can break the spell of anorexia/bulimia, it becomes possible to identify and defy the requirements of anorexia/ bulimia. Compliance with the demands of anorexia/bulimia often include the requirements:

a. to work the body to exhaustion, typically between 15-18 hours per day,
b. to engage in mindless, compulsive rituals often involving cleaning, folding, menu preparation, etc.,
c. to attend exclusively to the needs and feelings of others without a thought for oneself,
d. to reject loving relationships, including those with family members in favor of isolation/exile or relationships which promote their servitude and degradation,
e. to reject pleasure and the satisfaction of any desire,
f. to measure every action against the "curse of the idea of perfection" and continually fail, and
g. to subject themselves to severe self-blame and self-punishments, to vilifications such as "ugly," "worthless," "useless," "trash," etc., or to mortifications and mutilations of the body.

As the person defies the tyrannical dictates of the anorexic/bulimic "deathstyle," she begins to call into question the anorexic/bulimic threats that had previously compelled her to acquiesce. Defiance and repudiation can take place in any of those areas of a person's life over which it has been established that anorexia/bulimia had extended its influence. The following are examples:

> "When I first saw you, I only knew it as saying to me the moment I put food in my mouth that I was bad and deserved to be punished." (Julie)

> Anorexia has left me to a certain extent with eyes–in that I can see her and her 'ridiculousness'–but she has her anorexic hand gripped so tightly around my heart and won't let go. . . . Anorexic demands allegiance through a ceaseless taxing of your flesh, energy, and self-love. She is a cruel, merciless, vindictive bitch." (Rebecca)

During this stage, people often report connecting with feelings, appetites, and desires that anorexia/bulimia had anesthetized. They report moving in the direction of self-acceptance and away from self-denial and self-punishment.

Once the thinking and doing of anorexia/bulimia have been identified, these can be contrasted with their anti-anorexic/bulimic counterparts. The person is faced with the dilemma of living through two alternative stories: an anorexic/bulimic story with its associated subplots (self-hatred, unworthiness, perfectionism), lines of action (living for others, self-recrimination, self-denial, self-starvation, physical torture, mindless rituals) and outcome (death), or an anti-anorexic/bulimic story with its associated subplots (worthiness, self-appreciation, being a pleasure to oneself and allowing oneself pleasures), lines of action (self-nurturance, assertion, mutual relationships) and outcome (freedom, creativity, happiness, and compassion). These distinctions emerge from the play of what Tomm (1991) refers to as "bifurcative questions." Here are some examples, excerpted from a therapeutic letter I (D.E.) wrote.

> You informed me you refused to go along with anorexia's 'commands,' even though it attempted to blame you for everything. How was it possible at this particular point for you to be so disobedient and defiant of anorexia? How were you able to trust in your thoughts, ideas, opinions, etc.? Do you think this was something of a milestone in your struggle with anorexia? Does it tell you that you are making some headway? Can you see a future for yourself up ahead and is that future a 'concentration camp' or your freedom? If you were to attend to your own pleasures, appetites, desires, thoughts, ideas, etc., how do you think you might develop differently? What would an anti-anorexic personal development look like to you? Feel like for you? Be like for you?

6. Deconstruct Anorexia/Bulimia

The commands and dictates that lie behind anorexia/bulimia can be "unpacked" and brought forward for inquiry and contest. The outcome of this can be referred to as "seeing the light," "unmasking anorexia," "exposing anorexia," "undoing anorexia's ruse," etc. The taken-for-granted realities and practices of anorexia/bulimia can be further subverted by situating them in cultural, historical and gender contexts. Persons can be invited to reflect on how they became recruited into anorexic/bulimic realities and practices. Through this deconstructive process, anorexic "truths" become far less compelling, and persons are far more able to entertain anti-anorexic/bulimic realities and alternative modes of relating to self and others. The following is excerpted from a letter to Rosemarie, aged 23 (3/5/92):

> When I inquired if you had UNMASKED anorexia, you told a remarkable unmasking story. But before you did, you made me realize that unmasking anorexia 'is crucial . . . it's the crux of the matter.' Permit me to re-tell your story: 'I had had a fight with my parents. The fight heralded several pro-anorexic days. Because straight after a fight, I can't eat. It's like a button being pushed. I was tremendously upset and decided to hide down by the pool in the back yard. I then saw this ugliness that scared me witless but at the same time, I was able to face it. I really identified it as an evil spirit. I felt its grip . . . its bite. We were locked in combat for between a quarter and a half hour. It started with panic and guilt over what I had eaten over the day. Physically, I was feeling sick. I felt a gut dread . . . an unfocused dread. But then for the first time, I was able to see anorexia as *an influence* I had placed my trust in. I saw for the first time its true face. I had never seen anything so hideous. It's a monster . . . black with indistinct features. It was more an emotional concept–MY TORTURE! It did manifest itself as a force of being . . . an evil power. I got the feeling I could oppose it. I struggled with it in hand to hand combat. I prayed to strengthen my resolve. I won that fight but it wasn't a fight that was all mine.'

7. Attend to Anti-Anorexic/Bulimic Thoughts, Feelings, and Actions with Both Curiosity and Enthusiasm

When persons have anti-anorexic/bulimic thoughts, feelings, and actions they can be understood as "unique outcomes" (White & Epston, 1990, pp. 55-63). Persons can be helped to perceive the significance of these "unique outcomes" by inquiries relating to (1) how they were able to achieve them, (2) the implications of these events in their fight against anorexia/bulimia, (3) what this says about them as persons (e.g., their intentions, values, beliefs, personal qualities, etc.), and (4) how an alternative future could become possible through these developments. At the same time, anti-anorexic/bulimic knowledges, actions, slogans are documented and added to the archive of The League or circulated through The League for commentaries.

RECLAIMING A LIFE AND MAKING AN APPEARANCE IN IT

8. Attend to Person's Identification and Expression of Previously Obscured Thoughts and Feelings Deemed by Them to be Descriptive of Their Subjectivity (Personhood)

Anorexia/bulimia encourages people to become invisible to self and others, physically and emotionally. When people turn against and refuse to engage in anorexic/bulimic practices, previously forbidden emotions such as anger, dependency, and vulnerability return. Persons must cope with anorexia-influenced fears that these feelings and desires will prove to be overwhelming or burdensome for others or will provoke rejection or attack. This has to do with the person substantiating herself *as a person* rather than as an insubstantial bodily object. Associated with this is the recognition of and entitlement to feelings, appetites, desires, opinions and thoughts. This will obviously impact upon not only what they consider they deserve, but even what they require in a relationship. Often existing relationships are subjected to very severe challenges and many of these are either ended, deferred, or revised. These relationships are now eligible for redescription as abusive, one-sided ("all take and no give"), degrading, master-pet, etc. Distinctions can be drawn around an anorexic and an anti-anorexic relationship: What would each entail and how would each party to either experience it? Hope for liberation is deepened and people start reclaiming their future visions and dreams, although there is often considerable grief for what has been lost. So-called relapses are now viewed as the inevitable cost of fighting for one's life. These times can be utilized as opportunities for reviewing strategies and renewing anti-anorexic/bulimic offensives. They are no longer cause for despair. The therapist might even respond to such events with relish rather than disappointment or concern.

> D: Do you think there is such a concept as 'anti-anorexic/bulimic daughter-father' relationships?
>
> J: I think there is such a thing as an anti-anorexic father-daughter relationship. I think such a father would instill, somehow or other, a sense of self-worth in his daughter and treat her as a valid individual with legitimate thoughts and feelings of her own. . . . With my father, I often feel I am not really there or that he is unable to recognize and acknowledge what is important in my life. . . . I agree with Lee (a member of The League) saying that anti-anorexic father-daughter relationships would be equal ones. My father was always domineering over my mother. He was never wrong in a disagreement nor would he even accept that there could be another point of view. I definitely believe that if I felt a sense of impact or effectiveness and felt I really existed, anorexia's grip on me would be greatly weakened or perhaps never have got hold of me in the first place. (Jane, aged 22)

The person's increasing capacity to identify and tolerate strong feelings (both positive and negative) in the present can be compared to anorexia/bulimia's refusal to allow this in the anorexic/bulimic "past," however recent. The therapist should attend to persons' developing capacity to believe in their feelings, desires, thoughts, opinions, etc., or to "know one's heart and mind," "connect heart and body" as significant moments in opposing anorexia/bulimia (e.g., "Do you think if you make more room for you in your life, there will be less room for anorexia in it?"). Space should be made in the therapy for the elaboration of these "self-discoveries," (e.g., "What are you learning about the nature of your pleasures that anorexia previously had forbidden you to experience?" "When you told anorexia to 'shut up' and instead you listened to your own voice, what did you say to yourself about the delight and satisfaction you provided for yourself eating that peach?"). This fosters a sense of progression and renewed hope.

9. Search for the Foundations of Current Anti-Anorexic/Bulimic Capacities in the Person's Recent and Distant Past

By establishing a "history" of the qualities, attributes, and "know-how" which underlie the current anti-anorexic/bulimic achievements, these aspects of the person can be integrated into an alternative story of strength, power, blameless innocence in protest of evil, etc., and liberation from that evil. This alternative narrative or story recognizes and validates these qualities, attributes, and knowledges, reinforcing the likelihood of their endurance and performance.

10. Externalize Anorexia-Encouraged Fears of Interpersonal Rejection or Attack in Response to Self-Expression and Assertion

Positive responses from others (including the therapist) to persons' self-expression and assertion (e.g., responses that contradict the dominant story about relationships) can provide a basis for challenging impoverishing views of relationship. Persons can be invited to evaluate relationships from an anti-anorexic/bulimic perspective, (e.g., "What do you imagine your sister would say if we asked her if she found you more companionable when there was less of you in anorexic times, or now that there is more of you as a person?" "Now that you have decided to take a stand for your rights, do you find that people are still treating you like a dog–as you described it–or more like a person? Which is your preference, now that you have had a taste of both relationship styles?").

POST-LIBERATION

By this time the person has a secure, self-embracing anti-ano-rexic life-style and has clearly separated herself from anorexia/bu-limia, although the anorexic/bulimic voice can still be heard. There is no requirement whatsoever for a *perfect* anti-anorexia/bu-limia; if anything, imperfection becomes almost an article of anti-anorexic/bulimic faith. Kati (aged 32), for example, when asked to develop an anti-bulimic measure of anti-bulimia came up with the following: "You vomit whenever you feel like it without feeling guilty" and laughed. Great emphasis is placed on caring for one-self physically and emotionally, learning about one's desires, appetites, etc., and coming to respect and believe in one's own thoughts and opinions. Concern for the ways and means that per-sons start expressing themselves and their abilities is high. The therapist is unrestrained in the pleasure s/he takes in the pleasure the person is taking in herself and the world around her. Out of context, many of these first events would seem trivial, for instance, "the first pleasure bath," or "the first cup of coffee in which you didn't feel required to serve everyone else first and yourself last," but they are surely not. Self-appreciation now replaces self-hatred/ torture, etc., and much of that can be attributed to the defeat of anorexia/bulimia.

11. Invite the Person to Elaborate Their Story of Struggle Against and Liberation from Anorexia/Bulimia and Circulate This Story to a Wider Audience

The elaboration and writing up (or any other means of documen-tation) can be accomplished through interviews in which the person is invited to serve as an anti-anorexic/bulimic consultant to other persons resisting anorexia/bulimia in their lives. Family members, friends, and other significant persons can be provided with the same accounts of this new narrative for their reference. This often heals many of the breaches of relationship that anorexia/bulimia fostered through either the person's feelings of unworthiness as a friend/rel-ative, etc., or the frustration and irritation others felt watching help-lessly as the person perished in front of their eyes.

12. Ritually Celebrate the Person's "Liberation" from Anorexia/Bulimia

A celebration can be used ritually to mark a person's arrival at a new status in life, and to further authenticate their new social identity. Much use is made of the "consulting your consultants" protocol described in Epston and White (1992). Another ritual is the "handing over" ceremony in which an anti-anorexic veteran is invited to join us and present the incumbent with The Anti-Anorexic/Bulimic League T-shirt. The recipient is asked to remember all those women executed by anorexia, all those languishing in the private "concentration camps" throughout the Western world, and is requested to walk forward into her own "freedom" and if it suits her, to speak out against anorexia/bulimia and all those beliefs and social practices that support it. The mood is lightened when The League's logo is revealed to them on the front of the T-shirt: A circle inside of which is the word DIET with a slash bisecting the "T."

FROM THE ARCHIVE OF THE ANTI-ANOREXIA (BULIMIA) LEAGUE CORRESPONDENCE BETWEEN FRAN MORRIS AND DAVID EPSTON

The following is a partial record of an anti-anorexic (bulimic) therapy in the form of letters, authored by DE and authorized by FM. Fran referred herself, having had DE recommended by her sister. At the time of our first meeting, she was considering self-execution, given how she had experienced and was experiencing her life as unendurable punishment and torture. The letters record meetings that were held on 4/29/92, 5/22/92, 6/8/92, 7/13/92 and 8/13/92.

(Note from the editor of the Special Volume: Unfortunately, because of space limitations, it has not been possible to publish the entire correspondence. David Epston has generously consented to allow a portion of the correspondence to be published although we both feel that this does violence to the integrity of the work that he and Fran did together. However, I felt that it was important to make the work available to readers of this book.)

With explicit consent, written notes are zealously taken throughout each meeting. I favor verbatim recording so that the person's voice can stand on its own in the letters (White and Epston, 1990). Letters are written up immediately after a session and sent to clients along with copies of any audiotapes made of the sessions. Fran Morris, when interviewed about her judgment as to the part the letters played in her liberation, deemed the letters to have been 90% responsible.

It is the co-authors' decision to allow these documents to stand on their own and for themselves without being framed by professional discourses which analyze them.

1. 4/29/92

Dear Fran,

You reassured me that "I want to fight for my right as a human being and woman to be!" You said you were seeking "liberation" from the "concentration camp" of anorexia/bulimia where you were put, without trial, in 1969. Even if you had murdered two or three people, you would have done your time by now and be walking the streets as a free person. Why is it that your human rights have been abrogated? Why have you been imprisoned? Are these questions you are willing to entertain? Is your freedom something you believe you are entitled to? More importantly, why is the "concentration camp" of anorexia invisible to its inmates and to the wider community? Do you wish to join The League in its mission to make the "camp" along with that "power" that set it up in the first place? But first things first!

The League is interested and concerned about the latter because you have survived anorexia longer than anyone we know. For that reason, we accord you a special respect and sympathy. Anorexia has not been able to kill you off and despite it, you have been able to make something of a life for yourself. Svetlana referred to it as "a small death": others a "living death," but you seemed very much alive. It got me wondering how you have been able to keep something of yourself from its grip. And by no means has it turned you mindless or "zombie-like" as Jacky described it.

From an anti-anorexia point of view, I gave considerable significance to your comments: "Also it's only recently that I've even begun to feel what things I do want to do; and what my needs are. I didn't know I had needs until three years ago. Or I knew I had needs but I didn't know what those needs were, let alone know how to ask for them to be met. I was a doormat!"

Now this was particularly relevant, given your description of your training as the dutiful, eldest daughter with an even more dutiful mother, burdened by six children and a workaholic/alcoholic doctor-husband. And you had all been deracinated from your home country. You told me you had no choice but to take up the "good girl" role by your mother's "right hand." At times, you felt the mother to your mother at the same time as being trained to serve men and ask nothing of them. You summed it up: "Don't bother Daddy!" and "Be a doormat!" As you said, you set to work in your life being "all out for everyone else." And you followed in your mother's footsteps here as "she did everything for everybody else."

Is it any wonder, you and everyone else overlooked you? Did you sense your mother's despair and longing, something she wasn't allowed to express, (even to herself)? She was to do her duty as a doctor's wife. How do you think your father conceived his duties to his wife? Was she expected to soldier on as if she didn't have any needs or desires or appetites of her own? Did your father expect himself to deprive himself of his desires and appetites or did he satisfy them in his own ways? It seems inevitable, given your circumstances, that you might conclude: "I didn't want my mother to have all this problem . . . I wanted to ease her load." Did you feel required to take her burdens onto your own young girl's shoulders? Is that where you got your education in "subservience," "self-denial," and "selflessness?" Feed the men and starve yourself!

How do you imagine anorexia was stalking you as you were growing up? Looking back, do you think you were living in its shadow, before it really darkened your life? Am I right in thinking that you have four sisters and anorexia has only claimed the lives of two of you? Or better put, half of your sisterhood? How did your other two sisters escape? Would you be even willing to wonder how they made their escape? Do you think this therapy might engage them in its inquiry? What would be the most pertinent questions to help them remember the information that might guide you out of this hell on earth? And if your sisterhood becomes avowedly anti-an-

orexic, what contribution could that make to bringing your other sister out of the "concentration camp" that she, according to you, remains blind to?

Fran, did your anti-anorexia commence when you refused your recruitment into the "perfect wife and mother" role and started making demands on your husband of fifteen years? Fran, there must have been some preparation for this action. It just could not come out of the blue.

What were the foundations for your anti-anorexia? What paved the way for it? Could you go back and trace the history *of this resistance? How would that history be different from the history of anorexia in your life? Which history would you prefer to associate yourself with? And might you consider on behalf of yourself and others in The League who will come after you to write it up, all the better to appreciate it and see if it predicts any more initiatives on your part? If you look back and see where you have come from, it often guides you in your next steps. That is my experience and that of many others in The League. . . .*

Fran, I know I don't know you well but I have met other women on "death row." I believe that you are further along the way than you can appreciate because you have had no one to share that experience with, no "map" to tell you where you are and how far you have come. If I am any judge you are more than half way. By saying this, I in no way want you to think I am diminishing your suffering, oppression, and torture. It is just my considered opinion, having watched many liberations over the past seven years, that you are doing well! However, there is an anorexic ruse that could betray *your progress. Let me inform you what it is. Anorexia's last ruse is to accuse you that you are not doing anti-anorexia perfectly or "good enough." It might then tell you: "So you might as well give up and return to my loving but lethal embrace." It might also attempt to convince you that you are not perfect enough for anti-anorexia, or that anti-anorexia is too good for you. There are probably some others it will try on you, so BEWARE!*

I very much look forward to reviewing the above with you at our next meeting. I enjoyed making your anti-anorexic acquaintance.

Yours anti-anorexically,
David

2. 5/22/92

I rang Fran several times before our next meeting on the 5/22/92 to reassure myself of her well-being. She informed me that she was "hanging on!" At our next session we were joined by a "reflecting team" (Andersen, 1987), hastily recruited from all those attending an Advanced Intensive Training Program/Seminar. The impact of their reflections, according to Fran, was so profound that she demanded a written version of their comments.

3. 6/8/92

Dear Fran:

What an anti-anorexic day today was! There was so much you had to tell me and I don't feel the following really will do justice to the joy you radiated. You informed me that there was an "embryonic feeling of being free . . . now I feel I want to not binge and throw up and I want a normal course of living." You said that this was related to what you described as "a shift inside of me" and that shift was following from your decision that you had a right "to be on the planet," "get real and honest," and that "anorexia just had to get out of my life." You had seen through anorexia too, alleging it to be "a form of deception."

Then we got to wondering how you had construed as a little girl that you were to be held responsible for your mother's weight gain following your birth. And how by holding yourself responsible as the guilty party, guilt coached anorexia in your life! This must have been a burdensome thought, knowing how weighed down by life your mother already was. Your mother's weight gain had to do with her pregnancy with you which added 28 pounds to her weight. You came to believe, in a young girl's way, that "I destroyed her self-image by making her fat." No wonder, "I hated seeing her tired . . . I took on so much . . . I wanted to give her some relief." But, in fact, guilt started to operate in your life and "I felt guilty I couldn't do more." You thought you might have, quite unconsciously, even exceeded your mother in terms of giving. At times, you even took up the role of "acting mother" and acknowledged that "it was difficult to give up the reins."

If your mother realized that guilt supported anorexia and that you felt guilt for having made her fat, do you think she would require you to do penance or do you think she would say such guilt was unnecessary and unwarranted? Do you think your mother would subscribe to anorexia's torture, punishment, and near execution of you for this selfsame "guilt?" What do you think the connection between this guilt and perfection is?

Still, as you put it, "I reached a point where I can't take it anymore." And, in fact, you came to the conclusion, moreover, that "I didn't want to do it anymore . . . I'm bored with it." You informed me that "it (anorexia) makes everything into a ritual and an obsession that has to be done 150% perfectly." Previously, you had "acquiesced" to anorexia but today you came up with an anti-anorexic slogan: "ACQUIESCENCE IS TO ALLOW ANOREXIA TO ANNIHILATE YOU." When I inquired as to how you had been so defiant to and subversive of anorexia, you came up with some striking examples of your anti-anorexia. You had been deliberately doing different behaviors, like not going for a swim, not allowing anorexia to coerce you into exercise, and, in fact, are starting to believe that your "life is free."

You are now, according to you, 75% free of anorexia and all that that entails. You are feeling a "new energy . . . my own soul energy" and no longer in the grip of the "black spectre." You were of the opinion that "anorexia has held my self away from me" and had the effect of divorcing you from your very own self. You have opposed this divorce by reuniting mind, body, soul as a woman-person.

You informed me that "I am staying a lot more in the present moment and just enjoying being with no strings attached, no guilt, just freedom." Fran, how did you cut the strings on guilt? How did guilt keep you from your life up until the point at which you severed your connection with it? Did your mother saying you weren't to blame have anything to do with this? Did turning 40 and knowing that you had martyred half of your life have anything to do with it? Do you think you were entitled to the second half? You now are finding that "my energy is coming from inside out" rather than being tyrannized by anorexia. Does this suggest to you that there is more of you on the inside and that you are no longer so vulnerable to the surveillance and tyranny of anorexia?

Fran, beware of anorexia's last ditch stand. If other accounts

from those who have liberated themselves are anything to go on,
prepare yourself for some desperate moves to undo your anti-an-
orexia by telling you that you aren't good enough at it, it's too good
for you, or you are unworthy of anti-anorexia, and the only course
you have open to you is anorexia's "fatal embrace."

As spokesperson for The Anti-Anorexia League, I invite you to
your freedom and you are most welcome to join us. When you do, it
will have a special significance for us because you have suffered
longer than any of us. For that fact alone, you are especially wel-
come.

I look forward to reviewing your anti-anorexia at 3:00 p.m., the
16th of July.

> *Yours anti-anorexically,*
> *David*

4. 7/13/92

Dear Fran,

In my absence, anorexia seemed to have departed your body,
admittedly, in a very strange way. I am wondering if this didn't have
a lot to do with your making the connection between "guilt" and
"perfection." "Because I felt so guilty, I had to make it up by doing
everything 150% perfectly." You thought that this realization has
assisted you in your unmasking of anorexia, even though as you put
it, "I'm still in the middle of it." Fran, you may be in the middle but
you are no longer muddled. In fact, you say that some clarity "has
come about through a very strong glimmer of light" into the dark-
ness of a life lived according to the requirements of anorexia. You
concluded that you "can now separate anorexia from me." When I
asked what you imagine would have become of you if you hadn't
done so, you replied: "If not, I wouldn't have been here" and
anorexia would have claimed another woman-victim. You realized
too that you had grown up "full of worry and fear of not being good
enough." Still separating yourself from anorexia "was more of a
feeling rather than being able to put it into words." But you thought
that "getting to have a close connection with a Divine source" was
another. You considered a "political focus" was a third possibility.
You summarized: "I have chosen to carry a legacy of what women

have been left with and are doing about it." You realized that you now have a mission of your own: "to free myself as well as others."

When I inquired as to some of the sources of these developments, you thought that the question: "HOW COULD I HAVE CAUSED IT ALL?" was crucial to your calling guilt into question rather than trying to satisfy its requirements of you to lay down your life to it. In fact, you thought of late you were "pretty free of guilt" even though its legacy is still with you in the practices that it has encouraged you to do all your life: for example, "apologizing all the time to the point of apologizing for my existence," "minimizing and putting myself down" and "people-pleasing."

You provided me with some evidence of that in the incident with your employer and how you were able to assert yourself so as to be able to attend this appointment. You had to admit this was certainly a "break-through." You realized too that "I am enjoying being with myself and not binging . . . I can sew, write, be there for others." You were even able to watch a movie. How's that for ANTI-AN-OREXIA!

In addition to separating yourself from anorexia, you have taken this "unmasking process" a step further by "seeing what was anorexic behavior and what was me." When I asked if you could provide me with some instance of anorexic behavior, you came up with "exercising to the point of dropping" and contrasted "choosing to exercise for fun or choosing not to" as an anti-anorexic form of exercise. Denying your needs was anorexic while the acknowledgement of your needs and not feeling guilty for doing so was anti-anorexic.

We then put our heads together and came up with some questions you might like to revise or amend and send to your sisters.

(1) "Why didn't you live your life according to guilt the way I have? I felt so guilty about our mother's lot in life and thought I had to carry and be responsible for everyone's burdens. I think I did this in part because our parents weren't there in terms of emotions because they themselves didn't acknowledge the legitimacy of their own needs. Our mother was a door-mat and our father was a workaholic/alcoholic.

(2) Were you at any time in your growing up or adult years beset by guilt? If so, how did you prove your innocence to yourself? Were you in any way like me driven by perfection?

(3) Do you think over-eating is connected to the same set of circumstances as under-eating (anorexia/bulimia)?

(4) Was your independence and aloofness your means of escaping a life of self-punishment and self-torture? Please advise me.

(5) You get a kick out of life and always seem to land on your feet. How have you taken advantage of life more than being taken advantage of by others? Please advise me.

(6) What was your experience of life in our family just before I got taken over by anorexia (1970-1)? Would you be surprised if I told you that for me, then, anorexia was a sort of reprieve from my experience living in our family.

Please help me with this, my beloved sisters."

Yours anti-anorexically,
David

5. 8/13/92

Dear Fran,

Well, what can one say but "Congratulations!" for walking away, a free woman-person, from the "concentration camp" of anorexia in which you served 23 years of a very precious life. As you put it so well, "Some of the anorexia is in the past . . . not all." And when I inquired how you had made this possible, you suggested a number of ways. Firstly, you are no longer "working hard at letting it go" but instead have adopted an anti-anorexic policy of relaxation and peace. You did mention that this has led you to permit yourself more substance in the form of seven pounds and that that has not scared you or panicked you. Do you think you deserve to have more substance as a person? You are even allowing yourself "to go to bed earlier" instead of anorexia burning you out. You now have "time for people . . . I am not so isolated." When I wondered what your new friends might see in you, you found it too new to answer that. However, I am still wondering. You are no longer going along with anorexia's demands to "be too fussy . . . I don't burn myself out. . . ." And you went on to describe yourself anti-anorexically: "I am now care-free," after 23 long years of being care-worn. You have even become so anti-anorexic that "I am not getting so worried about organizing things . . . I am more sponta-neous." And to top things off: "I am putting people ahead of perfec-tion . . . they can accept me as I am . . . I feel a self-acceptance . . . they can like me, warts and all."

"So where now?" I asked. "Now that you are looking, have there been some opportunities that you are seizing upon, some doors that you now can see are open to you?" And sure enough there were. You informed me that "I now can do a yoga teachers' training course . . . 2 years ago, I didn't." Do you think if you were still an inmate in the "concentration camp" of anorexia that you would be embarking upon what you refer to as "a good medium" for me. Fran, do you think the torturing is over?

You acknowledged that "anorexia comes up now and then . . . but I am now able to go with MY gut feeling not anorexia's gut feeling." And then you told me that "I am no longer counting calories." Nothing could be more convincing than that.

I wondered how much time anorexia used to take up in your day and you mockingly replied: "48 hours." How much of your life have you rehabilitated," I inquired. You said, "98%." Even here, Fran, you refused to go along with perfection by giving anorexia its due. "What was it like to have your life back after 23 years of imprisonment?" You said with some delight: "It was hard at first . . . now I am feeling like normal . . . I have a lot more freedom." And this has meant that you are now able to express your creativity. In fact, you thought you had retired from over-responsibility.

You have also started revising your relationships with your par-ents. You remembered something which you considered was "a real plus." You were able "to be relaxed around eating at home." From an anti-anorexic point of view, Fran, what do you make of this? What does this tell you about the person you are becoming? What does this suggest to you about a new kind of relationship with your mother and father?

You then generously agreed to review your anti-anorexia with us. Here are some of your considerations as to what might constitute an anti-anorexic therapy:

1. *Knowing there is someone else who had similar experiences so I didn't feel strange.*
2. *Seeing the progression when my mind sorted out who I am and what anorexia is.*
3. *You accepting me as a person and not someone who is sick or diseased.*
4. *Finding out I could be free.*
5. *The political slant opened up new doors and made me aware of how much I* and other women *have been manipulated into being overpowered by men. It made me see too how I was part of a big machine and I wasn't guilty for it all. I had got caught up in a web of power.*
6. *You created a therapy for me/us . . . you weren't working to a set pattern. I wasn't being type-cast.*
7. *The letters were food for thought . . . things I could go back to.*

And when I sought your advice as to how one might experience oneself as more care-free, your counsel was as follows: "Accept yourself as you are. Accept yourself as a human being without a label. I would trust you in whatever you do. And I would advise you not to try too hard to get free. There is no right or wrong, only is-ness."

You thought too that going free of guilt was "a crucial part" of your anti-anorexia. You described guilt as "a metal helmet sitting on my head" and then you came to know that: "I wasn't responsible for it all." And that had quite an effect on you: "Guilt dropped. A heaviness went. I felt myself taking responsibility for what I needed to take responsibility for. I can now stand back, be detached, and not get embroiled."

You also thought that going "public" was an important part of your anti-anorexia and we worked out that anorexia is "shame" and that anti-anorexia is "pride," anorexia is "secret" and anti-anorexia is "public." I forgot to tell you that our Anti-Anorexia/Bulimia t-shirts are on the way. Do you want me to order one for you? Better yet, what if I present one to you on your "freedom day," a day I will look forward to whenever it comes. I believe you will know it when it arrives. In the meantime, I will be digging out some recipes to bake an anti-anorexic "freedom" cake to mark the occasion.

Freedom is yours!
David

Follow-Up

Fran and I met on two occasions early in 1993 (2/3, 2/15).[3] Since we had last met, Fran had made a "voyage of discovery," traveling to places she had never been before in New Zealand. When she returned, she informed her parents that "you haven't lost me but I've found myself." She had decided that "it's okay to be here on this planet . . . I let go a heap of the past . . . I feel I'm flying . . . before I was locked in fear." She informed me she was "tending herself like a young plant . . . I want to feel that deep rooted sense." She then amazed me by informing me she had decided to sell her house and travel to the U.S. to do yoga training and "reclaim" her life. When I inquired as to her recent developments in her relationship to anorexia/bulimia she had a great deal to say. I will let Fran's words conclude this paper.

"I was very close to death in the early stages but I didn't even realize it. I have thought of ending my life seriously two or three times to the point where I was going to get a doctor's prescription and end it all. That's when I came to you. You saved my life, old bean! You were one of the first people who took me as me and didn't treat me as sick. You offered the essence of unconditional acceptance . . . no weight requirements, I didn't have to stop vomiting . . . no rules . . . no blackmail. You were not perpetuating the prison. You helped me to see I could get out of my own prison."

"I am now saying 'hello' to anorexia and asking it what it has got to say to me. Why are you separating me from being who I really am? Sometimes now, it doesn't answer back. It's frightened of losing its power. But it hadn't realized we could work together. I want to learn from it. I am integrating those parts of me that have been separated. It's happening. I've always had the feeling of being split. I've often felt 'I'm not me . . . I'm separate . . . I'm different . . . divided into various aspects of my personality.' However, this led me to either kill myself or get on and live. I don't deserve this crap anymore. I really want to be and be here and to accept that it is okay for me to be human."

"Yes, I am getting better. I came to a realization that my feelings were just feelings, not me. I am not my feelings . . . I am not my thoughts."

"I am still dealing with the fear that if you eat, you'll never stop. The body has its own wisdom and I have to believe in it. Anorexia had canceled that out. I will get balance. I no longer give it power by obsessing about it."

"I would advise other women that there is hope. It can seem like you try everything and nothing works. But all the time you are doing the spade work and there comes a point when all that pays off. Then there is a shift . . . I couldn't tell when it would come. Anorexia started for me when I was 17 and I'm now 40. But I allowed for change. I kept on telling myself I could change. I kept learning who I am and I am still learning and will do so until the day I die. All my compulsions (swimming, walking, cycling) are just gone. It just happened. An almighty shift in focus. An abrupt change of focus. There is a newness about me. I am having a new relationship with myself."

AUTHOR NOTE

Acknowledgment is given to the Anti-Anorexia/Bulimia League of New Zealand: This work in general owes a great deal to fifteen years of Michael White's work in this area (White, 1983; 1986) and the colleagueship, lively discussions over lunch, and encouragement of my partners at The Family Therapy Centre in Auckland, Johnella Bird and Joan Campbell.

NOTES

1. This day-long workshop was presented at the New Zealand family Therapy Conference, 1991, Auckland. Since then, I have read two papers strongly advancing a parallel point of view (Gremillion, 1992; Swartz, 1987).

2. The "voice" of anorexia/bulimia is often gendered and "it" is typically given male status. According to feedback, this has provided one of the most provocative and helpful questions: "Why is the 'voice' of anorexia/bulimia most often gendered male?"

3. Judith Myers Avis (Professor of Family Therapy, University of Guelph, Guelph, Ontario, Canada) spent a week at The Family Centre as the Dulwich Scholar in February, 1993. She allowed The League to reflect on itself by interviewing many of its current membership and me. We are grateful for her contribution and her encouragement.

REFERENCES

Allen, L. (1993). Politics of therapy–An interview with Michael White. *Human Systems: Journal of Systemic Consultation and Management.* 4:19-32.

Andersen, T. (1987). The reflecting team: Dialogue and meta-dialogue in clinical work. *Family Process.* 27(4):371-393.

Bakhtin, M.M. (1994). *Problems of Dostoevsky's poetics.* Minneapolis, Minnesota: University of Minnesota Press.

Binswanger, L. (1958). The case of Ellen West. In R. May, D. Angel, & H.F. Ellenberger (Eds.), *Existence.* New York: Basic Books.

Epston, D. (1989). *Collected papers.* Adelaide, S.A.: Dulwich Centre Publications.

_____ (1993). Internalizing discourses versus externalizing discourses. In S. Gilligan & R. Price (Eds.) *Therapeutic Conversations.* New York: W.W. Norton.

Epston, D. and White, M. (1992). *Experience, contradiction, narrative and imagination.* Adelaide, S.A.: Dulwich Centre Publications.

Epston, D., White, M., & Murray, K. (1992). A proposal for a reauthoring therapy: Rose's revisioning of her life and a commentary. In S. McNamee & K. Gergen (Eds.) *Therapy as social construction.* London: Sage Publications.

Gremillion, H. (1992). Psychiatry as social ordering: Anorexia nervosa, a paradigm. *Social Science and Medicine,* 35(1):57-71.

Halliday, M.A.K. (1978). Antilanguages. In M.A.K. Halliday, *Language as a social semiotic: The social interpretation of language and meaning.* London: Arnold.

Madigan, S. (1992). The application of Michel Foucault's philosophy in the problem externalizing discourse of Michael White. *Journal of Family Therapy.* 14:265-279.

Platt, C. (1992). Formerly chronic bulimics' perspectives on the process of recovery. (Doctoral dissertation, California School of Professional Psychology–Berkeley, Alameda, 1992). *Dissertation Abstracts International, 53,* 3162.

Robertson, M. (1992). *Starving in the silences: An exploration of anorexia nervosa.* North Sydney: Allen and Unwim.

Swartz, L. (1987). Illness negotiation: The case of eating disorders. *Social Science and Medicine.* 24(7):613-618.

Tavris, C. (1992). *The mismeasure of woman.* New York: Simon and Schuster.

Tomm, K. (1989). Externalizing problems and internalizing personal agency. *Journal of Strategic and Systemic Therapies.* 8:16-22.

Tomm, K. (1991). Personal Communication.

Tomm, K. (1992). Personal Communication.

White, M. (1983). Anorexia nervosa: A transgenerational system perspective. *Family Process.* 22:255-273.

_____ (1986). Anorexia nervosa: A cybernetic perspective. In J.E. Harkaway (Ed.) *Eating Disorders*. Aspen Publishers: Maryland.

_____ (1989). *Selected Papers*, Adelaide, S.A.: Dulwich Centre Publications.

_____ (1984). Pseudo-encopresis: From avalanche to victory, from vicious to virtuous cycles. *Family Systems Medicine.* 2(2):150-160.

White, M. and Epston, D. (1990). *Narrative Means to Therapeutic Ends*. New York: W.W. Norton.

A Letter to David Epston

Peggy Penn

Dear David,

Commenting on your work joins me with many others in a kind of pride of curiosity, for many of us are eager to fully understand the remarkable progress you have made in treating anorexia with correspondence as an important component. Your letters to clients do, as Howard Moss (1985) describes, "bit by bit," break from conventional therapeutic discourse as they extend the dialogic space, *out* of the session. Marilyn Frankfurt and I have been describing the dialogic space as a circumstance where we treat each other intersubjectively; a space where no one is treated like an object (Penn & Frankfurt, 1994). This dialogic space is present first between you and your clients and later among the members of the Anti-Anorectic League.

We write to clients only on special occasions; they do the writing; they write to others and to themselves in the form of journals, notes, letters, records of dreams, poetry, etc. We understand their writing as an artifact of their own change as well as a representation of the therapeutic union. Paul Ricouer writes that any story, once told, is illusory, that is, constructed (Ricouer, 1984). More so when written,

Peggy Penn, MSW, is a senior faculty member of the Ackerman Institute, 149 East 78th Street, New York, NY 10021.

The poem "Beach Glass" is being reprinted with permission of Simon & Schuster, Inc. from SECOND NATURE by Howard Moss, Copyright ©1967 by Howard Moss. Originally appeared in The New Yorker.

[Haworth co-indexing entry note]: "A Letter to David Epston." Penn, Peggy. Co-published simultaneously in the *Journal of Feminist Family Therapy* (The Haworth Press, Inc.) Vol. 7, No. 1/2, 1995, pp. 97-101; and: *Cultural Resistance: Challenging Beliefs About Men, Women, and Therapy* (ed: Kathy Weingarten) The Haworth Press, Inc., 1995, pp. 97-101; and: *Cultural Resistance: Challenging Beliefs about Men, Women, and Therapy* (ed: Kathy Weingarten) Harrington Park Press, an imprint of The Haworth Press, Inc., 1995, pp. 97-101. *[Single or multiple copies of this article are available from The Haworth Document Delivery Service: 1-800-342-9678, 9:00 a.m. - 5:00 p.m. (EST).]*

© 1995 by The Haworth Press, Inc. All rights reserved.

in fact one could say, and we do, that the writing becomes an act of interpretation.

We feel the use of writing expands the session's language and the client's voices. In our case, these written "texts," letters or journals, return to the session visibly changed from the at-home reflections. In your case, the texts change with each exchange of your correspondence. Through writings then, the session "travels," and in so doing, becomes a metaphor for the alternative knowledge traveling *into*, transferring into, our lives and relationships.

Another thing we share is a contagion of questions. Some of yours I am especially responsive to, for instance, "What did you see that you had already known in a wordless way?" This question has a strong aesthetic appeal for me because, in fact, you are persuading someone(s) to find the pleasures of their *own* intuition. It respects clients as self-knowers and sees them as people who are expanded through their exchanges with others.

A clear difference between your work and ours is your boldness in challenging the life and death structure in the anorectic discourse through using what you describe as "opening a linguistic space," i.e., the correspondence. This life and death struggle reminds me of two things: the title of a book and a poem by the poet, Anne Sexton, called, *That Awful Rowing Toward God,* (the story of an Awful struggle), (Sexton, 1975) and, Mikhail Bakhtin's writing on "Carnival Knowledge" which he describes as an underlying folklore knowledge that conspires *at all times* to challenge life and death (Bahktin, 1981). You David, joined with your client(s), construct a challenge *to death* but not to life. In so doing you are able to sever that ultimately final polarization and construct with your clients an alternative self-knowledge. The Anti-Anorectic League becomes a place to strengthen and contain this new discourse through a culture of written texts that characteristically resist privileged cultural practices. It offers a different cultural morality; one that confirms and enjoys women, one that is different from a morality that oppresses and subjugates women.

We are similar in several other respects. To begin with we both regard social process as a construction of knowledge that is open to multiple discourses and we both regard therapy as an act of imagination and empathy. I like Roy Schafer's (1983) comment that a therapist needs "empathizing stamina," an apt description for what you, my friend, have in abundance! Do you feel, as we do, that this empathy toward clients results in the *client developing empathy for herself and consequently for others?*

I include imagination because therapy is invented *each* time it moves from one written text to another. For example, I believe we share the view that through writing we can effectively address cultural redundancies which you can't do by just remembering conversation. Moreover, writing is a socially constructed act since in order to write you experience *both* positions, that of the sender and that of the receiver. To write to someone you must fictionalize the "other," imagining their intentions, feelings, etc., for what you write is shaped by the other's anticipated and imagined response.

A difference of interest: you focus on revolting against the anorectic self by strengthening the advocate self in an almost instrumental way, to, in your words, challenge, "the totalizing description of anorexia." In your stance the anorectic self must be warred against, externalized as an enemy–for it fools you, torments you, deceives you, etc., and its practices must be resisted in the name of the advocate self! When you join your client these acts of resistance become advocate-self enhancing. Together then you are able to do two things: combine acts of resistance with the discovery of alternative self-knowledge.

In contrast, we talk about the co-existence of multiple selves that have representative voices which in combination can achieve narrative multiplicity, or the participation in more than one self story. This emergence of multiple selves depends on changing a negative inner monologue to internal dialogue. Once the internal conversation is taking place we see the client's conversation with others change.

So many questions remain: are there ways you involve the family besides in the letter? How long do you write to a client . . .? How do you sense women understand the meaning of a man participating so strongly in their liberation? etc., etc.

I could continue but I'm suddenly remembering what my grandmother used to say, "Your imagination is running away with you again!" That's my cue to stop writing and look forward to your reply.

Affectionately,
Peggy

Beach Glass

Mr. Calava rises at five
A.M., the first on the beach, but not
Because he's crazy about the sea.
He's crazy about beach glass. He has
Two thousand pieces
At the latest count.
An industry of idleness,
He's a connoisseur of broken glass.

Sucked candy bits as hard as lava,
The shards are no longer sharp
In every shape and every color–
The commonest are white and brown:
Harder to find are blue and green;
Amber is rare; yellow rarer;
And red the rarest of all. The sea's

A glass-blower who blasts to bits
Coca-Cola and Waterford,
Venetian as well as Baccarat,
And has carefully combed its five-and-ten
For anything made of glass. It isn't
Fussy. It knows that everything
Will be pared down in the end:

Milk of Magnesia bottles honed
To sky-blue icy filaments,
And smoky cordial bottles from
Brazil–sunglasses of an eclipse.

Mr. Calava's kaleidoscopes
Are kept in apothecary jars,
As if the sea were a pharmacy
Of lozenges and doled them out
Without a prescription, especially
For Mr. Calava, who firmly believes
The best things in life are free.

But what the sea has relinquished it
Has relinquished only in part. You know
How childish it is in its irony.
The jig-saw puzzle is here. But then
Its missing pieces are still in the sea.
Not all the king's horses and all the king's men
Could ever put it together again,
Though—chip by chip
And bit by bit—
Roualt could make a King of it.

Howard Moss

REFERENCES

Bakhtin, M.M. (1981). *The dialogic imagination*. Austin, Texas: University of Texas Press.

Moss, H. (1985). *New selected poems*. New York: Atheneum.

Penn, P. & Frankfurt, M. (1994). Creating a participant text: Writing, multiple voices, narrative multiplicity. *Family Process*.

Ricouer, P. (1984). *Time and narrative*. Chicago: University of Chicago Press.

Schafer, R. (1983). *The analytic attitude*. NY: Basic Books.

Sexton, A. (1975). *That awful rowing toward god*. Boston: Houghton-Mifflin.

The Discourse on Thomas v. Hill:
A Resource for Perspectives
on the Black Woman
and Sexual Trauma

Jessica Henderson Daniel

SUMMARY. The analyses of the Thomas v. Hill hearing is used to provide perspectives on the inclusion and exclusion of the black woman in the discourse on sexual trauma and women. The paper examines: the history of sexual trauma of the black woman by white and black men; the conflict in the black community about the hierarchy/status of race vs. gender; and the social constructions (old and new) of the black woman. *[Single or multiple copies of this article are available from The Haworth Document Delivery Service: 1-800-342-9678, 9:00 a.m. - 5:00 p.m. (EST).]*

The Judge Clarence Thomas Senate Confirmation Hearing was the major media event in October 1991. Millions tuned in to witness

Jessica Henderson Daniel, PhD, is Assistant Professor of Psychology in the Department of Psychiatry, Harvard Medical School, as well as Co-Director of Training in Psychology and Associate Director of the Adolescent Training Program, Children's Hospital, Boston.

Correspondence may be addressed to the author at 295 Longwood Avenue, Boston, MA 02115.

Supported in part by Project #MCJ-MA 259195 from the Maternal and Child Health Bureau (Title V. Social Security Act), Health Resources and Services Administration, Department of Health and Human Services.

[Haworth co-indexing entry note]: "The Discourse on Thomas v. Hill: A Resource for Perspectives on the Black Woman and Sexual Trauma." Daniel, Jessica Henderson. Co-published simultaneously in the *Journal of Feminist Family Therapy* (The Haworth Press, Inc.) Vol. 7, No. 1/2, 1995, pp. 103-117; and: *Cultural Resistance: Challenging Beliefs About Men, Women, and Therapy* (ed: Kathy Weingarten) The Haworth Press, Inc., 1995, pp. 103-117; and: *Cultural Resistance: Challenging Beliefs About Men, Women, and Therapy* (ed: Kathy Weingarten) Harrington Park Press, an imprint of The Haworth Press, Inc., 1995, pp. 103-117. *[Single or multiple copies of this article are available from The Haworth Document Delivery Service: 1-800-342-9678, 9:00 a.m. - 5:00 p.m. (EST).]*

© 1995 by The Haworth Press, Inc. All rights reserved.

Anita Hill's graphic testimony alleging trauma in the form of sexual harassment and Judge Clarence Thomas' strident responses as he sought a seat on the Supreme Court of the United States. Across the country, the hearing was the topic of discussion with a two-volume quality, both in level and number. The depth of the emotional responses suggested indeterminant degrees of complexity and confusion. Some people felt the issue was veracity–who was telling the truth. For some it was a race matter and for others, it was gender. For still others, the hearings produced a discomfort of undifferentiated affect. Some wanted to avoid the matter but were snared in the webs of strongly held opinions. In particular the black community, rich in its heterogeneity, seemingly was immersed in a sea of intense exchanges.

Newspapers and magazines as well as books presented the multivariate opinions and analyses of the hearing and the details of the testimonies. However, one book, *Race-ing, Justice, En-gendering Power,* edited by Toni Morrison (1992) will be the basis of this discussion because the writers' analyses can be related to black women and sexual trauma.

Trauma is a pervasive topic for mental health providers, law enforcement personnel, members of the judiciary, and social policymakers. The recent proliferation of articles and books documents the extent to which trauma has been and continues to be dominant in the lives of large numbers of people. For women, four forms of trauma: child abuse (physical and sexual), domestic violence, rape, and sexual harassment have been most prominent. Disclosures and discussions on talk shows provide the impetus for people to reveal and report traumatic experiences both in the privacy of their therapy hours as well as to friends, law enforcement officials and other media consumers (electronic and print). Docu-dramas and news programs chronicle and bring to life the mortality and morbidity data.

The recognition of trauma in the lives of individuals who present for therapeutic services has become an integral part of numerous training and continuing education programs for mental health professionals. Therapists are urged to be cognizant of and sensitive to the myriad traumas to which individuals have been subjected during their lives. Recognition of trauma is presented by authorities in the field as essential to the initiation of a healing process.

Mental health service consumers represent a range of age, social/ cultural groups as well as social classes. In order to provide services which meet the needs of consumers, practitioners are challenged to understand the different contexts in which consumers' lives are embedded. Many factors, including demographics, influence the particular traumas experienced as well as their sequelae.

The content of a therapy hour is significantly influenced by the knowledge base of the service provider as reflected by her questions, comments, and interpretations. As a consequence, to some degree, what is both heard by the service provider and shared by the mental health consumer are influenced by the provider's construct of the social context of the consumer's life. This paper seeks to expand the cognitive lenses of providers as they work with black women.

It is important to note that even when trauma is placed in a social-political context, race can either be excluded from the discussion or discussed in stereotype. An example is the highly acclaimed *Trauma and Recovery* (Herman, 1992). While Herman acknowledges the relationship between psychological traumas and affiliative political movements, e.g., shell shock-combat neurosis and the anti-war movement as well as sexual-domestic violence and the feminist movement, both racism as a psychological trauma and the affiliative Civil Rights Movement have been omitted from the book. A black person is mentioned only once in the text, in the stereotypical role of the black male as rapist of a white woman. A critique (Daniel, 1994) using the Ethical Principles of Psychologists and the Code of Conduct (APA, 1992) found the work to be in violation of Principle B: Integrity; Principle D: Respect for People's Rights and Dignity; and Principle F: Social Responsibility.

While the focus of the paper will be on the black woman and sexual trauma, the underlying premise is that a range of women should be an integral part of any presentation on sexual trauma. Using the analyses of the Thomas-Hill Senate Hearing, the discussion will delineate factors which may impede both the receptivity to narratives about sexual trauma in the lives of black women and the disclosure of traumatic sexual experiences by black women.

Anita Hill's allegation of sexual harassment informed many about the vulnerability of women in the work place. But the hearing had a powerful impact on the black community, raising many issues critical in the lives of black men and black women. The hearing highlighted the complexities of the intersection of race and gender.

When sexual harassment involves a black woman alleging sexual victimization by a black man, historical factors and intra-racial conflicts contribute to the significance of the allegation. Thus, the analyses of the Thomas-Hill hearing provide insight into: the history of sexual trauma of the black woman by white and black men; the conflict in the black community about the hierarchial status of race vs. gender and the subsequent silencing of the black woman; the social construction of the black woman; and, the reconstruction of the black woman.

HISTORY OF SEXUAL VIOLENCE

McKay (1992) in a summation writes "the story begins with the rape of African slave women by white men across the Middle Passage and on the plantations of the South, connects with the black men who, during the Civil Rights Movement boasted about practicing that assault on black women before attempting it on white women, and joins itself to the white and the black men who even now, as the treatment of Anita Hill by Clarence Thomas and the Senate Committee demonstrated, continue to assault them with impunity" (p. 278).

Darlene Clark Hine (1993) describes the sexual victimization of black slave women by masters, overseers, and other white men who "could and did rape slave women at will. The consensus is that at least 58 per cent of all slave women between the ages of fifteen and thirty were sexually abused by white males. Rape had the added advantage of producing new slaves and thus enriching masters while satisfying white men's carnal desire" (p. 341).

Black women who write fiction have been important sources of published narratives about the sexual traumas of black women. It is striking that such pain had to be fictionalized for presentation, thus leaving the veracity of the patterns of abuse open to question. Black women's traumas have become entertainment. J. California Cooper's short story, *Red-Winged Blackbirds* (1987), depicts sexual vulnerability. A black girl is sexually harassed by a white boy. While she manages to get away from him, she makes the mistake of informing her father first rather than her mother. Her father confronts the father of the boy. The results are profound: the burning of the family home and the deaths of both parents in the house fire. The girl is left an orphan. The message is clear. Black girls and women learn to keep such sexual harassment from the males in their lives lest the men seek to either avenge or stop the exploitative behavior. Such action might result in the death, torture or maiming of the black man. The silence was maintained to keep black males alive. It was understood that to tell was possibly to issue a death sentence. Sex and violence, threatened and experienced, have been powerful control measures in the black community.

Clearly, slavery did not mark the end of the sexual exploitation of black women. Attractive black adolescent females have been sent to the North by caring and fearful parents to keep them from being exploited by the men in the homes where they would be employed as domestics. Their concerned parents realized that they could not protect them from being the prey of white men who were aware that there were no consequences for the sexual assault or rape of a black woman in most communities in the South.

The autobiographical play, *From the Mississippi Delta* (1993), by Endesha Mae Holland includes a scene depicting her rape in the home of a white family where she had been hired as a babysitter. The white woman literally led her to the bed of the rapist. As a girl, black and poor, she was powerless to defend herself from the assault. In the play, she notes that while only 11 years of age at the time of the rape, she stopped being a girl that day. It was 1955. The Holland story suggests the probable existence of other black women who have suffered such sexual traumas as children and adolescents in their personal histories.

It is important to note that generally white men are neither accused nor convicted of the sexual traumatization of black women. As important is the fact that no man, black or white, has ever been lynched for the sexual harassment or assault of a black woman (McKay, 1992). Unfortunately, the history of the black woman in the United States remains untold which explains why Judge Clarence Thomas was not initially challenged on the legitimacy of his allegation of "high tech lynching." However, black women have been lynched or have had loved ones lynched, with them sometimes witnessing the atrocity.

Crenshaw (1992) describes the differences in the punishment meted out to black men when they rape white women versus black women. She notes that the pattern of punishing black men more harshly for raping white women than those accused of raping black women is an example of discrimination against black women. She suggests that black women are victimized by the racial hierarchy which does not see black women as equal to white women when they are the victims of sexual trauma. Black women are double trauma victims: of sexual and institutional racism.

The intersection of sexual harassment and black culture was confused by the comments of Orlando Patterson, a Harvard professor who indicated that black women like the so-called flirtation which Judge Thomas allegedly engaged in with Anita Hill, referring to it as "the down-home style." While black women may have learned to live with such advances from black men, there is no evidence to suggest that they enjoy such exchanges or that they consider those behaviors to be true to the culture (Crenshaw, 1992). Sexual harassment and assault are not a "black thing." Psychological injury is the outcome of such behavior when black women are the victims, regardless of the race of the perpetrator.

The historical vulnerability of the black woman to sexual trauma by both white and black men is clear. However, given the invisibility of the black woman in the history of the United States coupled with negative stereotypes, her sexual victimization can be trivialized.

RACE vs. GENDER AND THE SILENCING OF THE BLACK WOMAN

The separation of the black woman into black and woman rather than an integrated "black woman" has created many dilemmas for the black woman and those who seek to provide services to her. McKay (1992) notes "for all of their lives in America, whatever the issue, black women have felt torn between the loyalties that bind them to race on one hand, and sex on the other. Choosing one or the other, of course, means taking sides against the self, yet they have almost always chosen race over the other: a sacrifice of their self-hood as women and of full humanity, in favor of race."

Anita Hill was portrayed as being disloyal to the race and even treasonous by disclosing the alleged harassment by Judge Clarence Thomas (Crenshaw, 1992; McKay, 1992; Painter, 1992). She symbolized the black woman who conspires with the white man against the black man, i.e., the pawn of white men (Stansell, 1992). What she did was an embarrassment to the black community (Crenshaw, 1992). Furthermore, she was "acting white" because that is the way that white women behave toward white men (Swain, 1992).

Veracity was not the critical variable but rather it was racial solidarity (Crenshaw, 1992). The message was clear: black men who are deemed to be successful are not to be subjected to potentially embarrassing and career threatening accusations by black women. As too few black men are "successful," those who are deserve to be supported without question. Further, accusations are likely to reinforce the negative stereotypes of the black man as, in this case, sexually threatening and worse yet, such disclosures may make him vulnerable to prosecution and incarceration. The consensus is that both the penal and judicial systems are particularly cruel and unfair to black men. Since all black women are aware of the above, they should, therefore, be protective of the race, i.e., black men.

The critical consequence is the silencing of black women lest they incur the wrath of the black community. The costs, i.e., defaming and racial banning, may be perceived by many black women as being too high. As a result, some black women have been silenced about trauma involving high-ranking black men. The pressure for racial solidarity is intense. Middle-class black women are particularly vulnerable to silencing as they are more likely to be involved with successful or prominent black men. When the conflict is between race and gender, it is expected that black women will decide that race will take precedence. The result is gender silence (Crenshaw, 1992).

Nellie McKay (1992) notes for the record that "Anita Hill was not the first black woman to speak out in America. Contrary to what many others believe black women have never been silent, it is simply that often, in a racist-sexist disregard and even denigration of them, others do not listen, and, therefore, almost never hear their voices. From the poet Phyllis Wheatley in the eighteenth century, to Maria Stewart, Frances Harper, Harriet Jacobs, Anna Julia Cooper in the nineteenth century, to Ida B. Wells, Pauli Murray, and dozens of others—writers, teachers, preachers, and women bent on reforms and hundreds of twentieth century women from all walks of life and members of all professions—black women have always spoken loud and clear" (pp. 287-288). Crenshaw (1992) comments, however, that those with voice have been ostracized and branded as man-haters or pawns of white feminists.

Black women who struggle with the issue of disclosure about sexual harassment and abuse may be perceived as dealing with family (nuclear and extended) loyalty issues. They may, in fact, be struggling with the race-gender conflict and the possible negative reactions of the black community. Observations of Anita Hill's treatment indicate that the community reactions can be very strong and quite painful. In sharp contrast, white women who disclose do not risk being perceived as being racially or ethnically disloyal.

SOCIAL CONSTRUCTION OF THE BLACK WOMAN

Painter (1992) writes "as the emblematic woman is white and the emblematic black is male, black women are not as easy to comprehend symbolically" (p. 210). Black women have been invisible or suffered the consequences associated with cognitive incarcerations of negative stereotypes. Both impact on whether black women can be perceived as victims of sexual harassment or sexual assault.

The stereotypic images of black women generally fall into the following categories: mammy, welfare queen, over-sexed Jezebel (Painter, 1992), and Sapphire (Links, 1993). The media have been the primary sources for images of black women in American society.

The black woman as mammy is the woman who takes care of everyone. Hollywood promoted the figure of the all-caring mammy who was the functionary—her value determined by her functions as maid in the homes of whites. Her personal needs were not acknowledged. In the movies, she had no life, although the reality is that many black women who worked as domestics in the homes of whites had full lives as wives, mothers and active women in their communities. The maid as mammy continues to exist today. She is the necessary but unseen and undervalued child care worker, hotel worker and hospital service worker. These women are the underpaid, invisible people who are important in making the lives of other people comfortable but who are portrayed as void of affect or value. As depicted in *From Aunt Jemima to Attorney Claire Huxtable* (Links, 1993), Hollywood's presentation of the black woman is of a person more attentive to the needs of whites than to her own. This black woman is asexual.[1]

The second image is that of the welfare queen. Clarence Thomas portrayed his sister, Emma Mae Martin, in this role. However, the facts indicate that she was on welfare for a short period of time and in reality throughout her adult life had been a "two-job holding minimum-wage-earning mother of four" (Painter, 1992). Her brief tenure as a welfare recipient allowed her to care for an ailing aunt who provided child care for her so that she could work (Painter, 1992). Individuals on welfare are generally seen as parasites of the government who do not make contributions to the society. They drain the economy; have many children, just to collect money; and inhabit the housing projects whose most notable products are the criminals who terrify all the "good" people. They are the loose women who are sexually irresponsible. The stereotype is one of a moral and economic drain on the society, i.e., people of questionable value. Their behavior creates perpetrators.

The third image is that of the over-sexed Jezebel who is perennially sexually available or the instigator of sexual encounters. She is portrayed not as the victim but rather as the wanton being (Painter, 1992). If she is always ready for sex, she cannot possibly be raped or sexually harassed.

The fourth image is that of Sapphire from the Amos n' Andy television program (Links, 1992). Sapphire is the figure who demeans the black man. Also, she is the hard and harsh image, the cold "I can take care of myself" image. Racist stereotypes that black women are tougher than white women and thus not injured by the same practices which injure white women reinforce the historical lack of protection of black women (Crenshaw, 1992). Can she be a victim of sexual assault when she can protect herself so well?

In essence, the stereotypic images depicted on the various cinematic-electronic wide screens, surrounded by reinforcing stereophonic sound, have effectively rendered even professional listeners, blind and deaf to the humanity of black women. Crenshaw (1992) points out that "even when the facts of our stories are believed, myths and stereotypes about black women influence whether the insult and injury we have experienced is relevant or important." The determinants of sexual trauma in this color context are hierarchical. The social constructions of black women mean invisibility, devaluation and lack of entitlement. The probable sequelae in the therapeutic relationships would be interpretations which dismiss or negate the experiences of black women. The clear result is a limited perception of black women as victims of sexual trauma.

THE RECONSTRUCTION OF THE BLACK WOMAN

What happens when the black woman does not fit the stereotypical images of black women? Some suggest that the black woman becomes invisible or she has to be reconstructed. Anita Hill, for example, did not fit any of the above stereotypes and therefore it was difficult for individuals to deal with her presentation.

McKay (1992) notes that she "had no believability" for the senators at the hearing so they had to make her the "delusionary opportunist." She was transformed from the brave woman to "the dupe of left-wing political activists or white feminists, vengeful lesbian feminist herself, or just an evil person bent on unwarranted revenge to ruin her former employer" (p. 286). The vilified woman of questionable mental status is not a likely candidate for the role of victim.

A second reconstruction of the black woman emerged as a result of the hearing: the "overachieving black lady." Lubiano (1992) notes that black lady may be an oxymoron. Further, she argues that Hill may be considered to be dangerous because she is a study in contradictions. She is a lady because of her class on the one hand and on the other hand she is not a real lady because she can clearly hold her own. Even Hill's delivery of her testimony was under scrutiny. That she was "quiet, direct and tearless" was interpreted as unfeminine and actually may have contributed to her "downfall." Anita Hill as the distressed black lady failed to behave in an acceptable manner. Another interpretation of the overachieving black lady is that she contributes to the strangeness of black culture where her disproportionate achievement somehow insures the underachievement of the black man. Perhaps she is the other side of the welfare queen who contributes to the undoing of the black community or a revisionist Sapphire. All of the above may have contributed to Anita Hill being demonized in that unfamiliar role. The overachieving black lady is an unlikely candidate to be a victim of sexual assault as she is not really a lady but in fact an aberration.

A third reconstruction involved the identification of Anita Hill as an affirmative action person. Lubiano (1992) suggests that the "aa" connection makes her the welfare queen's more articulate sister as both may be seen as the recipients of advantages and resources which are unmerited. The vilification of both is thus explained. The third reconstruction, that of the "aa" woman, can generate considerable affect about the employment and advancement of a black woman, a two-column entry in the race-gender body count. Her designation as victim may be problematic especially when her employment has placed others in a victim state. She is a perpetrator.

Finally, another reaction to Anita Hill was to de-race her. She was whited out so that she could be seen as a woman–namely a white woman. It was an option exercised by white feminists who were unable to tolerate the reality of her being a black woman. Crenshaw (1992) notes "content to rest their case on the raceless tale of gender subordination, white feminists missed an opportunity to span the chasm between feminism and antiracism. Indeed, feminists actually helped maintain the chasm by endorsing the framing of the event as a race versus a gender issue. In the absence of narratives linking race and gender, the prevailing narrative structures continue to organize the Hill and Thomas controversy as either a story about the harassment of a white woman or a story of the harassment of a black man" (p. 415). Black women who are de-raced have potential as sexual trauma victims.

Hill as the unknown entity becomes invisible, lunatic, the overachieving black lady, "aa" symbol or a de-raced woman, i.e., white woman. It appears that only in the latter construction, de-raced to be a white woman, can a black woman be seen as a potential sexual trauma victim.

The four commonly held stereotypes as well as the four newly constructed images singly and in combination can eliminate black women from being considered legitimate victims of sexual trauma. The images in the minds of both the therapists and the recipients of services who have been educated by the same media and educational systems conspire so that too many black women are without a place to heal from the pains associated with sexual trauma. Unfortunately, too few mental health providers have confronted the reality of the role of stereotypes of black women in therapy. Educated black women, saddled with the revisionist labels, are just as vulnerable as their less educated sisters. As a result, the voices of black women may be distorted by some listeners and by some women who themselves may accept the stereotypes or misconstructions.

CASE EXAMPLES

Case I–A young professional black woman sought therapeutic services to address self-esteem issues. Her initial focus on the educational and socio-economic achievements of both herself and her family portrayed a multi-generational black middle-class family. Inquiries related to a more broad-based family history including critical incidents and familial relationships (nuclear and extended) were met with some resistance. Her emotional pain was in sharp contrast to the glowing family portraits. Her pride in being from a line of strong powerful bright black women was evident. She was the third generation to be college educated. History of trauma–sexual or physical abuse was adamantly denied. However, in one session, after noting her slow progress in treatment, she casually stated that she had been raped, adding quickly, she was "over it." Her perception of the rape was that it had been her fault because she had been raised as a strong black woman who could take care of herself. Allowing herself to be raped was being disloyal to the family legacy of the strong black woman. She was ashamed. She had bought into the Sapphire image of the black woman. Her education and class had not protected her from internalizing the stereotype which did not allow for other possible perceptions of the rape. The disclosure marked the beginning of a healing process which included reframing her image of herself as a black woman. Her therapy provided opportunities to explore the stereotypic images of the black woman which may be detrimental to her self-esteem.

The situation was further complicated by the middle-class status of the black male perpetrator. She could not consider ruining his life by pressing charges against him, i.e., the Sapphire image coupled perhaps with the Jezebel image. While she did not press charges, she was able to understand her decision-making in the context of the race vs. gender dilemma faced by black women.

Case II–Another young professional black woman presented with "the blues"–not really depression, she insisted. She had relocated from the South to a Northeastern city which represented a culture shock. It was a move from a predominantly black environment to a predominantly white environment. She attributed her "blues" to racial isolation. Her colleagues and supervisors were all white. While they were friendly, she felt voiceless in the group, especially with the head of the organization. A racial history of the family yielded no significant data. However, when the Thomas-Hill hearing resurfaced in the news, she discussed her confusion about the hearing. In the course of her therapy hour she revealed that she had been sexually assaulted as a child by a powerful white man. She had never told, fearing that her otherwise mild-mannered gentleman father would have had an angry response which could have resulted in his death. After all, she explained, it was the South. Her silence was her effort to keep her father alive. When informed that her silence was not unusual, she noted that it made sense, now. Therapy became a safe place to talk about her victimization as a child and how that might impact on her relationships with white men in powerful positions.

CONCLUSION

A significant event in the society can have implications for the providers of mental health services. An example is the Thomas-Hill Senate Hearing where millions of Americans watched the exchange of accusations. But it was more than an exchange between a woman and man. It was an enactment of the intersection of race and gender. The analyses reviewed in this paper provide needed opportunities for mental health providers to gain understanding of the dynamics of race and gender in the lives of black women as they relate particularly to sexual harassment and sexual assault. Mental health providers need to offer a therapeutic context which is accepting of the voice of a range of black women who are able to be both black and female. Black women need to be in therapeutic settings in which negative stereotypes and injurious reconstructions are not dominant. Further, it is hoped that the ideas presented here will encourage mental health providers to include discussion of race and gender in their clinical work, presentations to colleagues, and their writings.

The necessary dialogues must not portray the black woman as only victim. By familiarizing themselves with the history of black women and their accomplishments (Hine, 1993), therapists will be able to provide the rich range of images of the black woman not just as survivor, but one who can and has thrived in a hostile environment.

NOTE

1. The author acknowledges the movement to reconstruct the image of mammy to be a more positive presentation of the black woman. However, for the current analysis, the more commonly held interpretation has been presented.

REFERENCES

Boston Chapter of Links Inc. (1993). From Aunt Jemima to Claire Huxtable. Images of African-American women on screen. (Videotape).

Cooper, J.C. (1987). Red-winged blackbirds. In: *Some Soul to Keep.* New York: St. Martin's Press.

Crenshaw, K. (1992). Whose story is it, anyway? Feminist and antiracist appropriations of Anita Hill. In T. Morrison (Ed.) *Race-ing, justice, en-gendering power.* New York: Pantheon Books.

Daniel, J.H. (1994). Exclusion and emphasis reframed as a matter of ethics. (Review of *Trauma and recovery* by Judith Lewis Herman) *Ethics and Behavior.* Vol. 4, No. 3.

Herman, J.L. (1992). *Trauma and recovery.* New York: Basic Books.

Hine, D.C. (Ed). (1993). *Black women in america: An historical encyclopedia.* Brooklyn, NY: Carlson Publishing.

Hine, D.C. (1993). "In the kingdom of culture": Black women and the intersection of race, gender, and class. In G. Early (Ed.) *Lure and loathing.* New York: Penguin Press.

Holland, E. (1993). *Mississippi delta.* Huntington Theatre. Boston.

Lubiano, W. (1992). Black ladies, welfare queens and state minstrels: Ideological war by narrative means. In T. Morrison (Ed.) *Race-ing, justice, en-gendering power.* New York: Pantheon Books.

McKay, N. (1992). Remembering Anita Hill and Clarence Thomas: What really happened when one black woman spoke out. In T. Morrison (Ed.) *Race-ing, justice, en-gendering power.* New York: Pantheon Books.

Morrison, T. (Ed.). (1992). *Race-ing, justice, en-gendering power.* New York: Pantheon Books.

Painter, N.I. (1992). Hill, Thomas and the use of racial stereotype. In T. Morrison (Ed.) *Race-ing, justice, en-gendering power.* New York: Pantheon.

Stansell, C. (1992). White feminists and black realities: The politics of reality. In T. Morrison (Ed.) *Race-ing, justice, en-gendering power.* New York: Pantheon.

Swain, C.M. (1992). Double standard, double bind: African American leadership after the Thomas debacle. In T. Morrison (Ed.) *Race-ing, justice, en-gendering power.* New York: Pantheon.

The Hill/Thomas Debate as Source for Understanding the Black Woman and Sexual Trauma: A Response

Elaine Pinderhughes

Jessica Daniel's use of the Thomas vs. Hill discourse as a resource for perspectives on the Black woman and sexual trauma does indeed expand the cognitive lenses of providers in their work with Black women. Her insightful examination of these issues illustrates how extreme is the entrapment of the Black woman in societal processes, crystallizes the complexities embodied in the intersection of race and gender. It is certainly true that there will still be exclusion of racial matters or inclusion of these matters via the use of stereotypes, confusing *even when* female trauma is placed in a sociopolitical context. I would go even further to insist that *it is precisely when* the context is sociopolitical that exclusion of race and trivialization of and mistreatment of the Black woman are likely to occur. The sociopolitical nature of the Black woman's role is explained by Bowen's concept of the societal projection process. He suggests that the dominant group in society can, through projec-

Elaine Pinderhughes, MSW, is Professor and Chair of the Clinical Sequence, Boston College Graduate School of Social Work.

[Haworth co-indexing entry note]: "The Hill/Thomas Debate as Source for Understanding the Black Woman and Sexual Trauma: A Response." Pinderhughes, Elaine. Co-published simultaneously in the *Journal of Feminist Family Therapy* (The Haworth Press, Inc.) Vol. 7, No. 1/2, 1995, pp. 119-122; and: *Cultural Resistance: Challenging Beliefs About Men, Women, and Therapy* (ed: Kathy Weingarten) The Haworth Press, Inc., 1995, pp. 119-122; and: *Cultural Resistance: Challenging Beliefs About Men, Women, and Therapy* (ed: Kathy Weingarten) Harrington Park Press, an imprint of The Haworth Press, Inc., 1995, pp. 119-122. [Single or multiple copies of this article are available from The Haworth Document Delivery Service: 1-800-342-9678, 9:00 a.m. - 5:00 p.m. (EST).]

© 1995 by The Haworth Press, Inc. All rights reserved.

tion upon a less powerful group, relieve anxiety and reduce tension in itself, thereby improving its functioning (1978, pp. 444-5). Identifying minorities as among those who are victims of this process, Bowen wrote:

> These groups fit the best criteria for long-term, anxiety relieving projection. They are vulnerable to become the pitiful objects of the benevolent, oversympathetic segment of society that improves its functioning at the expense of the pitiful. Just as the least adequate child in a family can become more impaired when he becomes an object of pity and oversympathetic help from the family, so can the lowest segment of society be chronically impaired by the very attention designed to help. No matter how good the principle behind such programs, it is essentially impossible to implement them without the built-in complications of the projection process. Such programs attract workers who are oversympathetic with less fortunate people. They automatically put the recipients in a "one down," inferior position and they either keep them there or get angry at them.

Visible at all levels of functioning in the social system, this process is evident (1) in the pervasive use of stereotypes held about Blacks, the Black family, the Black man and especially the Black woman–stereotyping being understood as a tension relieving mechanism; (2) in the use of these stereotypes to create environments such as ghettoes and suburbs where whites live in relative peace and tranquillity while Blacks and other ethnic minorities are constantly beset with chaos and disorganization; and (3) in the implementation of social policies such as the War on Poverty in ways that focus not on the social situations that create poverty but on the adaptive strategies that poor people devise to survive; and Affirmative Action that focuses not on the societal processes that create lack of opportunity, and thus lack of preparation on the part of so many minorities, but on the compensatory corrective measures as undeserved, unmerited and victimizing of others.

The existence of these dynamics has ensnared the Black female in a situation characterized by double entrapment. As tension relievers and anxiety reducers in the larger social system, she, her family and her cultural group are trapped in their projection process roles which channel anxiety and conflict to them and their communities while providing tranquillity and stability for the dominant group.

In her female role of nurturer, supporter, enhancer of others, she is expected to support, sustain and nurture not only the Black man who is likely to be unemployed, underemployed, or if employed, too often beset with threats to his self-esteem, but all family members, both nuclear and extended as well.

Moreover her nurturing, enhancing role extends also to her cultural group where she is expected to counter its lack of solidarity and work for its advancement. Thus she can be silenced, as Daniel suggests, by threats of ostracism, defaming and racial banning, for speaking out and failing to protect even her Black male abuser/harasser. Being trapped as a tension reliever, anxiety reducer for her own family and race–both of whom, in turn, must serve that function for the dominant group (including the white woman)–means that the Black woman's role in the larger social system is truly a nodal one.

An example of the seeming intractability of this nodal role is seen in Daniel's examination of the reconstruction of the Black woman's image whenever there is recognition that she does not fit the old stereotypes of mammy, welfare queen, oversexed Jezebel/prostitute and Sapphire. The new reconstructed images (as invisible one; lunatic; dangerous and overachieving; affirmative action product who victimizes others; and deracinated woman, i.e., white woman), have not freed her but instead maintain her in that tension reducing role. For, as Daniel suggests, none of these images permits her to be viewed with respect, allows her pain to be heard, or her sexual trauma to be placed in the larger discourse.

Her trivialization and mistreatment become understandable as part and parcel of the sociopolitical context that must be maintained to benefit others. For if she were to become respected, protected and visible in the full range of her selfhood, with open discussion of her abuse, she would no longer be sacrificing herself as a tension reducer for others. This would mean that the beneficiaries of her nodal position, the Black man, her family and the dominant group would have to give up the stability provided them at her expense.

This would require taking back their projections on her and finding a way to tolerate the systemic anxiety which her presence has helped them to control—not a likely scenario in the near future.

Daniel's clinical examples show the necessity for educating the Black girl and woman to the complexities of her nodal societal role. They also hint that insight assists in managing the associated ambiguity and contradiction that can be so entrapping.

I also believe that understanding the dynamics of this societal projection process, and the way in which her entrapment in that role provides stability and relieves anxiety, not only for the white man and the white woman but also the Black man, will prepare her for what she must do. It will help her to understand that declaring her refusal to choose between her race and her sex, and thus claiming both her humanity and her sense of self, and in daring to be both Black and woman, she may find herself in a very lonely place.

But she can come to see, as Daniel notes, that knowledge of history and of the Black woman's achievements assures recognition of those who have already accomplished this feat, surviving and even thriving. This vision can make that place no longer lonely but heroic.

REFERENCE

Bowen, M. (1978). *Family therapy in clinical practice.* New York: Jason Aronson.

Opening Therapy to Conversations with a Personal God

Melissa Elliott Griffith

SUMMARY. Systemic therapists are particularly aware that a person's sense of self is co-created in a social network of relationships and conversations with others. But often clients feel that their private and meaningful conversations with a personal God are unwelcome in the therapy conversation. If we consider this unspoken censoring as a form of professional oppression, though usually inadvertent, then we may see not only how we participate in oppressing but how we can participate in freeing our conversations. It is therapists' certainty that oppresses and constrains opportunities to hear the story as the client experiences it. I offer four certainties I have recognized in my own work and how, with the help of clients and research participants, these certainties have changed to wonder and creativity. *[Single or multiple copies of this article are available from The Haworth Document Delivery Service: 1-800-342-9678, 9:00 a.m. - 5:00 p.m. (EST).]*

There is no completely open conversational space in therapy just as there is no totally neutral therapist. Therapist and client are

---

Melissa Elliott Griffith, MSN, is an Adjunct Assistant Professor, Department of Psychiatry, George Washington University.

Correspondence may be addressed to her at 1855 Foxstone Drive, Vienna, VA 22182.

[Haworth co-indexing entry note]: "Opening Therapy to Conversations with a Personal God." Griffith, Melissa Elliott. Co-published simultaneously in the *Journal of Feminist Family Therapy* (The Haworth Press, Inc.) Vol. 7, No. 1/2, 1995, pp. 123-139; and: *Cultural Resistance: Challenging Beliefs About Men, Women, and Therapy* (ed: Kathy Weingarten) The Haworth Press, Inc., 1995, pp. 123-139; and: *Cultural Resistance: Challenging Beliefs About Men, Women, and Therapy* (ed: Kathy Weingarten) Harrington Park Press, an imprint of The Haworth Press, Inc., 1995, pp. 123-139. *[Single or multiple copies of this article are available from The Haworth Document Delivery Service: 1-800-342-9678, 9:00 a.m. - 5:00 p.m. (EST).]*

© 1995 by The Haworth Press, Inc. All rights reserved.

123

always opening and closing the doors to new places together, looking for that which has not been seen, listening for that which has not been heard, negotiating together the limits and the possibilities. My partner, James Griffith, and I are attempting to make the therapy space open enough for the most significant conversations to be heard and understood, and for the most significant others to be included in the construction of meaning, even when that significant other may be the Other, who is known by many names, whom some call God (Griffith, 1986; Elliott-Griffith & Griffith, 1992). If discourse is, as Bakhtin (1981) says, basically political, if story is made from many voices competing for space, then power is having space in the discourse. Justice, then, is when clients can tell their stories as they experience them, the only just censorship being that of protecting others from harm.

The space that this justice would create for clients to speak of their experiences with a personal God can be limited both by *proscriptive constraints*–that this God-talk is not to be spoken of here, and by *prescriptive constraints*–that God can and should be spoken of here, but only in a certain way. The secular psychotherapy culture may influence a therapist to impose proscriptive constraints inadvertently, while the religious counseling culture may influence a therapist to impose prescriptive constraints inadvertently.

This is not to say that a therapist's choice to limit spiritual talk is always inadvertent. Occasionally, therapists say that they intentionally avoid discussing any religious topics with their clients, "That is the business of the priest, not the psychotherapist." And clients say, "I prefer to deal with God's business in God's house."

However, most therapists recognize the significance of their clients' spiritual experiences and wish their clients could talk freely about them. This has been evident in many conversations with secular psychotherapists, pastoral counselors, and the multitude of therapists who, like myself, are influenced by both these cultures. Clients and persons who have participated in our research[1] have told us that they want to reflect on their spiritual experiences in therapy, and that they feel fragmented by attempting to delegate psychological, relational issues to conversations with their therapist and spiritual issues to conversations with their priest, rabbi, or pastor. As one working within the psychotherapy culture nestled in the Bible Belt, this is a relevant concern for almost every person I work with in therapy, since almost every person has, has had, or feels that he or she should have had a relationship with a personal God.

So why don't conversations about this relationship happen in therapy? Given that therapists, counselors, and clients want these conversations to occur, what underlying assumptions lead us, unaware, to constrain them?

THE ENTRAPMENT OF KNOWING

I had not seen Susan since two years ago when I had met with her and her mother in my role as family therapy consultant to a panic disorders treatment program. "I'm in trouble again. I didn't want to go back to the panic disorders specialist, because he would not ever meet with me and my Mama, but I knew that you would. I guess he thought I was too old for that, but what he doesn't understand is that Mama is the best support that I have, the only one who really knows. Anyway, I get the feeling he thinks I should see less of my Mama, not more, but my getting well really matters almost as much to her as it does to me."

Of course, she did not want to lock her mother out at a time like this, and why should she have to? I began to privately simmer with indignation. I could say that the steam of my indignation rose from my commitment to systemic family therapy or to the notion that it is the client's privilege to bring whom she wants to her therapy. But, honestly, the fire that made my pot boil was my own experience in mothering, and, parenthetically, my own experiences as a mother accompanying a child to a psychologist. I was thinking, "Where does this guy get off, deciding that Susan's mother would be bad for her, that she is overdependent, and that only he knows best about who should be involved in her treatment? Susan and her mother have solved many problems before he came along. Good for her that she has decided to forego the expert and keep her relationship with her mother!"

She interrupted my thoughts, "I brought you something." She pulled a book from her purse, something like *The Christian Answer to Anxiety*. I squirmed, not wanting to dishonor her but not wanting to be programmed by ideas I might find hard to swallow.

"So when I realized that I could not go to the specialist, I started reading this wonderful book that Mama got for me. I read and I prayed, and I decided to come to you. I don't know if you will agree with this man's methods, but he has some good sound Christian ideas. If I'm going to get over this, I will need all the support I can get, my Mama, you, and God."

I hesitated, fearing I could not satisfy Susan and remain true to myself. I thought of a perfect solution. I should refer her to a reputable local seminary-based counseling program that I thought might parallel the ideas of her book. "I don't know that I could learn and employ his methods, but since you find this to be so valuable, would you like me to connect you with a counselor who might have more expertise with this approach?"

"No, I don't want to do that. In fact, I called the author of this book in Oregon and asked him what I should do. He told me to come back to see you because I said I was comfortable with you. He even said that we didn't have to use his methods, that we could just take what we want to use and leave the rest. I'm pretty sure that we can work it out. I just know that I need to depend upon the Lord and that I can't do it alone."

Susan was asking me to include her God, not to be programmed by her book. She just wanted me to be interested. This was similar to her asking the panic disorder specialist to include her mother. It made sense. So whatever made me so hesitant? The selfsame kind of kneejerk thinking, I am embarrassed to say, that gave the specialist pause. When I saw the book title, I thought I *knew* about the God with whom she related. I *knew* that this was going to be an authoritative, inflexible, totally male God who would not only want Susan, but me, to be unquestioning and to submit to his authority. Because of what I thought I knew, I almost lost this opportunity to work with Susan, her mother, and her God, who actually turned out to be concerned, calming, and the One whose quiet, gentle voice she could hear the most clearly, calling her to self-acceptance and health.

This and many other cases repeatedly teach me that if "I think I know" the basic story of someone's experience with God, I am probably beginning to close off therapeutic possibilities. I then risk joining those forces of cultural oppression that would instruct and censor what could be spoken. Resistance to these forces is possible only to the extent that I can discover and depart from my own certainties.

James and I have been interested in this process of discovering "stories of certainty" that lure us into "already knowingness," away from curiosity and creativity. We hope to open these certainties to the refreshing breezes of curiosity and wonder, in which multiple realities can coexist and relationships can evolve. Both our clinical work and our research work (Tingle et al., 1992) have helped us to move from certainty to curiosity. Surely we have only begun to discover the "stories of certainty" that intrude into, oppress, and constrain the possibilities for conversations with God in therapy. Surely, other readers may still see certainties we continue to employ that we are unable to see. Or perhaps the reader may discover certainties of her or his own.

FROM CERTAINTY TO WONDER

I will offer some "certainties" we are beginning to recognize that we have held in our work and will then offer ways that we are finding to introduce curiosity.

Certainty 1: I Know What God Is Like for You Because I Know Your Religious Denomination

When Southerners meet one another for the first time, each person's denominational affiliation is often part of the initial exchange of information. This classification cues us into the worship style and behavioral code of that group. This established, one would be more likely, say, to invite the Episcopalian and not the Southern Baptist over for daiquiris. Of course, it could be that the Episcopalian was a member of AA and that the Southern Baptist enjoyed daiquiris, but a stranger would be more likely to learn this than a fellow Southerner.[2]

Likewise, we are cued into images of what God is like for that group. One is likely to imagine the God of the Southern Baptist to be a close, but strict, father, while the God of the Episcopalian to be a remote, but lenient parent. This is often as false as the assumption about who enjoys daiquiris.

Our research has born out the shallowness of these assumptions. For example, we could not find a correlation between measures of religious fundamentalism and the extent to which the God portrayed by the individual showed qualities of acceptance or flexibility (Tingle et al., 1992).

In therapy, stated beliefs or denominational group beliefs are also poor predictors of a person's experience of God. When I first met Thomas, I wondered if his religious doctrine would ever allow him to feel forgiveness. As he told me his story, I found myself wishing he were an Episcopalian, so that he might have a lenient God–but he wasn't. He was a loyal member of a Reformed Presbyterian Church. Members of this group believe in sanctification and obedience to strict moral code. They are known to be as clean and honest in appearance as in behavior.[3] Thomas felt unclean because of an affair with a married woman. His secrecy about it had separated him from his faith community and his God. According to his stated beliefs, he could not approach God until he was clean because "God cannot look upon sin." Yet he could not change his ways without God's help.

"I am in quicksand," he said, "and I did this to myself. There were warning signs all around–DANGER-DO NOT ENTER–but I went into the swamp anyway, willfully. Now I am stuck in the quicksand. The more I try to get out by my own efforts the deeper I get. It is a toxic place, too poisonous for any person to enter, and too filthy for God to even look on." As time went on we talked about his dilemma from many perspectives, all along wondering what God's perspective might be. Actually, he said, he knew the Lord would rescue him. He had before. It's just that he had seen such disappointment and weariness in the Lord's face. He couldn't ask him to make the sacrifice of coming to this vile place to save him. I could not see a way out of his bind.

Then one day he described an experience, like a very real daydream. In truth, his vision was as surprising to me as it was to him. He saw the Lord walking toward him, past the danger signs, boldly, into the swamp, to the muddy, smelly quicksand, bending down and lifting him up, carrying him in his arms to a cool, clear stream where he dipped and cleansed him, then carrying him out, with words of comfort, not of reproof.

"And what of the mud and the filth in that place? Did the Lord walk through it with disgust or did he walk above it, untouched by it?" I asked.

He paused to reflect. "He was in the midst of it, not above it, but it didn't seem to be a problem. I couldn't see him react to it at all because his eyes were on me."

"And did he look sad and tired?"

"No, he honestly just looked peaceful, genuinely happy to find me and to cleanse me and to give me rest."

The wonderful surprise to Thomas was not that his Lord would help in time of need, but that the Lord would come through the filth without disgust. With this new knowledge, he could reconnect with members of his faith community. He started by forming one new friendship there, that was neither dominated by a need to confess nor to hide. More recently, he has informed me that there are many trusting friendships that are now possible because he knows the grace of his Lord. With the new knowledge Thomas has given me, I can connect more creatively with other persons from conservative denominations, expecting to be surprised, rather than stifled.

Certainty 2: I Know What God Is Like for You Because I Know What Your Language About God Means

As we gather in churches to worship, we speak together the words of a liturgy, the common words that bind us together. Many persons in our city utter, "Our Father who art in Heaven," to begin the Lord's Prayer on Sunday morning. When asked what God is like, they might say "like a kind heavenly father," and we might then think that we know about their experience.

Our[4] research conversations suggest, however, that these words, though not false, are more like a door, and though the doors to different persons' hearts may look the same, the insides are wonderfully different. These are a few of the descriptions we have heard from persons we have talked with in research and in therapy (Griffith et al., 1992). Most persons had started their descriptions with "God is like a kind father," but when we asked further, we heard a wide range of images spoken in quite different ways. We found this question helpful in moving from certainty to curiosity: "In those moments when God is most real to you, when you know you are with God, what do you hear or see or feel that tells you what God is like?"

"Like a warm cocoon, enclosing me as the world falls in around me."

"Like an exasperated mother whom I have disappointed and been ungrateful to too often."

"Like an Olympic coach who does not model my task for me, but delights in my potential and pushes me to it."

"Like a nourishing, flowing river that comes to me, the parched dry river bed, and gives me life."

"Like a strict old grandfather, angry with my continual wrongdoing, who has finally turned his back on me."

"Like the silence in a deep, waterless cavern where I finally arrive after swimming down through a troubled lake."

"Like a nursing mama who is happy to be close to me and always has plenty of milk. As I lay my head on her breast, I feel her breathing and hear her heartbeat and I am calmed."

When we asked, "What human relationship in your life most reminds you of the one you have described with God?" some who had begun with a description of a kind father God did, indeed, recall their own kind fathers or grandfathers. Others who related to a kind father God associated to relationships with women:

"My mother, who kept calm and kept things in perspective."

"Our housekeeper, who taught me about love that lasted through hard situations."

"My grandmamma, who always had a lap available."

"My women friends who are closer than family, who confront me, encourage me, and support me no matter what."

"My other mamma, my Irish Catholic neighbor lady, who always had room at her table for one more, whose house was liberatingly messy and filled with laughter, who, when she gave of herself, became more, not less, of herself."

We have also become aware that there is no language therapists can employ–including the word "God"–that is free from oppressive connotations. One research participant, Priscilla, said, "I don't use the word God when I can avoid it. That's the word I used for the old "Thou-shalt-not" God who stifled me for so many years. That word almost makes me sit up straight at attention, be careful, not talk, and *certainly* not laugh. That word has nothing to do with the Spirit I know now, the Spirit inside me and surrounding me who invites me to open, to love, to create, and to laugh."

"But," she smiled, "if you really need me to, I'll say 'God' with you. Just remember that it's shorthand, not the real thing." It was not necessary for me to use it, though. Now we could find new language together.

I could not ever have known what the word "God" was like for her, nor any other word by knowing its dictionary definition, or even its common cultural usage. Language, as the hermeneutic philosophers have taught, is a way of being present with another person, a way of touching the other (Heidegger, 1971; Gadamer, 1976). To Priscilla, to say the word "God" was to touch her with a hard, cold thing, but to learn and to say her words–"Spirit" and "Light"–was to touch her with a strong, enveloping goodness; for her, "the real thing."

Certainty 3: I Know What God Is Like for You Because Your Image of God Is a Reflection of Your Early Attachment Figures

Object relations theorists propose that the God-image is a synthesis of parts of parental images (Rizzuto, 1979). We earlier described a feedback cycle that explained how such an image of God, drawn from early life sources, could remain stable over time (Griffith & Elliott-Griffith, 1992). These ideas could guide the therapist to maintain a story of certainty wherein the character of a person's God cannot transcend its resemblance to the character of the person's parents.

What interests us now, however, are not explanations for the stability, but the transformations, differences, unique outcomes that could never be predicted by these theories. These latter elements deconstruct our certainty, and questions based on these elements free us to be curious.

Carol came to therapy for help with extreme anxiety symptoms. She was a brave and determined woman, working three jobs to support herself and her daughter. I often privately wondered whether I could offer her anything in an hour that would be more helpful than the nap she appeared to need. "Must you work this hard? Could family or maybe bank loans help?"

"No, there is no help, and, yes, I am physically exhausted, but I can handle it."

As we talked more it seemed that this philosophy had served her well through a difficult life. Her inner talk seemed to go something like: "This is tough, but I'm tough too, and I can handle it." Or "If I can handle it, then I should handle it."

I wondered if, given a choice, this was a philosophy she would select to guide her life. Carol thought she would prefer in the future when making decisions to ask, "Am I comfortable with this?" and "Is it worth my time and effort?" But she felt it would be very difficult to change, since she received so much praise for her stamina. I began to wonder who in her imaginal dialogues (Watkins, 1986) might encourage her to seek a more comfortable life and who might bind her more into the "I can handle it" lifestyle. As she reflected on these questions, I asked where God might be in this debate. I knew Carol to be a spiritual person who was a sensitive, comfort-giving woman to her daughter and friends. I probably expected her to say that God would want her to stop suffering and to have rest and comfort.

Her reply jolted me. "Well, this must be how God wants it or he would change it. He would get some money to me, but obviously he doesn't want it to be any easier for now."

"So he wants it this way?"

"Yes, I think he could change it. I see him somehow getting money to my friends. But there are no family checks coming to me. There is no let up. I am suffering and so is my daughter. It's like he's saying, 'I know you can work very hard, harder than most people, so I know you can do this'."

"What is it like to hear these words from God? Do you tell him you're suffering?" I asked.

"It's lonely. I don't feel very close to him. I don't tell him anything. I'm not even sure he hears me."

"What do you sense from him, as he urges you to work hard? A tone of voice, a face, a posture? Could you show me?"

"I can't see his face, because his face is turned away. I can only see the side of it, like this," she demonstrated, standing erect, embodying a God with arms crossed, stonefaced, head turned away.

"What does that face mean?" I wondered with her.

"I'm not sure, either anger or disappointment. He doesn't tell what it means, but it feels awful to me."

We paused. I asked, "Has there been a human relationship in which you had this feeling of a face turned away, not knowing what it meant, but feeling awful?"

Her gaze drifted away. "Well, maybe with my grandfather. He was strict and very religious, but he was really good to me in lots of ways, the steadiest person in my life. I hated when he was angry with my cousins, though. He wouldn't say he was angry. He would just ignore them, not acknowledge them. Sometimes he would have gifts for the rest of us, but not for the ones he disapproved of. That was awful."

I did not say a word. In a flash, Carol was aware of the parallels. "Wow," she said, "that's pretty similar. I mean, intellectually, I believe this is not all there is to God, but that's sure how he is for me right now, way out there, not very concerned about me, but he has gifts for those others."

This was a point where I could have asked her what she believed, what she knew intellectually that was different than her experience, but, she had already said she *knew* this did not tell the whole story of God, yet still this was her experience. I was interested, not so much in what she knew, but how she knew, that, "This is not all there is to God." As with any relationship, one could assume that Carol's experiences with God were broader and more varied than could be captured by any single story, including the one about her grandfather. I asked then, not about similarities to the grandfather story, which seemed to be so limiting, but about times when her experiences with God were unlike those with her grandfather.

"Carol, has there ever been a time when you experienced God being with you in a different kind of way, a time where God surprised you?"

"Oh yes, I can remember a time very clearly years ago. It was after I had stopped drinking, not long after I became a Christian. I was facing so much, sinking deep into depression without the relief

I once had from getting drunk. One night I decided I had to go drink. I couldn't take feeling this bad anymore. I got dressed to go. I knew that the Lord would be disapproving of me, maybe angry with me for doing this wrong thing, so I didn't want to think about him. But I sat down before I left and turned and there was Jesus sitting by me . . . weeping . . . not weeping in a way to make me feel guilty . . . just sad for me, deeply sad that I was about to do something to hurt myself and that I was hurting. He just didn't want me to hurt. It was like he took my hands and we wept together. I didn't need to go drink then. In fact, it was then that I first was able to ask for help for the depression and got some therapy which did help."

I wondered what was possible in the presence of the Lord who wept with her that was not possible in the presence of the God who turned a face away. I also asked her, "If Jesus were here with you, now, weeping, knowing your suffering, how would he talk with you about your life, your hurting now?"

"I'm not sure, but it's enough to just have him near now. I haven't felt that presence in a long time."

Now, whether a person's description of God is generous or stingy, kind or cruel, like or unlike early attachment figures, I always ask, "Is there any other way you have experienced God, any way that surprised you?" Almost always there is. If the person would like to be more with God in this way, then this can be a point of curiosity, or time to delight in, to historicize, and to expand this alternative story (White & Epston, 1989).

It is still quite useful to hear the stories that people often relate about similarities between experiences with God and experiences with early attachment figures. But if such a story is unwelcome, it can become less constraining when known as only one of many stories of the person's relationship with God.

Certainty 4: I Know What God Is Like and You Need to Know God As I Do

All of the stories I have written here end with a person describing an encounter with a loving and accepting God, a God of grace. I remember these stories because I love them.

I must then always ask myself if I am imposing rather than

co-creating these endings: I hope not, for a God of grace imposed is still imposed. I learned this many years ago from Mary.

Mary was in serious danger of death from self-starvation, entrapped in a vicious binge-purge cycle. She knew that she needed inpatient treatment, but refused to consider it, not because she didn't want it, but because she felt she didn't deserve it, and that she didn't deserve to upset and worry and cost her parents more than she already had.

Mary mentioned that she had attended a church that was known in our city for its acceptance, although she had always sat in the back row. I hoped that going to that church might show her a God who deemed her acceptable and worthy of living.

"Do you ever talk with God about your dilemma about going to treatment?" I asked.

"Of course not. It's no use."

"Why? What would happen if you did?"

"God," she said with a bitter tone of sarcasm, "isn't talking to me these days."

I asked her if she could show me what that was like. She showed me Mary, seated on the floor, head down, eyes looking down and God, high up and far away, back turned completely to Mary, speaking these words grimly. "I have given you chances to change before, and you have failed. You have been selfish and stubborn. I have tried and tried to help you, but I have grown tired of you. You don't really want to get well and you have used up your chances with me." Her God never flinched, never considered turning to look at Mary. On questioning, she was very sure that was how God was and that any other experiences of God were now invalid. It was understandable, after all, since she was unlovable and unbearable.

I was horrified. I felt my body stiffen and recoil. I could not let her go on. I interrupted her. "No, Mary, that's not God! I know it's not! Don't you see?" I began to explain.

She turned me off with a bored cold stare and left the room. I don't know if she said with her eyes or her lips, "I didn't come here for preaching," but I knew I had betrayed her and been untrue to what I had promised the therapy would be about.

After that I listened and tried to understand. We didn't stop talking about God. I asked her with genuine curiosity what it was like sitting in the back row listening to descriptions of a God who would always forgive, yet finding a God who had become fed up and turned his back. "It's like a thick piece of glass is between me and the rest of the church, not sound-proof but feeling-proof glass. It gets thicker every week."

Then one day she came in with light in her face. "I'm ready to go inpatient. I need to take care of myself. I want to live. Lots of other people want me to live, too, even God wants me to live." I was happy, but stunned, "What happened? How can this be?"

"On the elevator coming up here, I ran into a little girl . . . well she's a big girl now . . . but she was little when I took care of her. I used to babysit her every day. I was so surprised to see her. It's been years."

"And what did she say?"

"Nothing, really. She just hugged me. She was so happy to see me. She loved me. She always loved me. I suddenly knew I was lovable. Somehow I knew God loved me too and that I must get well."

Mary did get well. I'm not sure how to understand the therapy as a part of it all, but she tells me it helped her get ready, and that what helped was that I didn't get scared and did not take charge of her life. She didn't remember how close I came to trying that, but I do. If my fear and knowingness had guided me to take charge of her life by preaching my own God, Mary likely would have been forced either to acquiesce to appease me or to leave the therapy.

It would not be true to feminist values to omit my context that gives births to, delights in, and struggles with this work. For me, this cannot be only therapy. It must be congruently connected with my own experience with God. When I hear experiences and descriptions that I feel could not be God, I want to defend and correct, as if someone were to have misunderstood my sister. I would have to defend her–to say, "No, you're wrong. She's not like that. She's kind and good." So will I not do for God as much as I would do for my sister?

The way I reconcile this dilemma is that, while my sister needs my defense and I need to defend her to strengthen and protect our relationship, the God I know does not need my defense. In the act of defending or silencing the attack of my client, I decrease possibilities for that person's intimacy with his or her God and intimacy in the therapy.

CONCLUSION

Undoubtedly, I will again become seduced into certainties, attempting in therapy to provide, rather than to co-create, the meaning of an experience with a personal God. The hope is that it is in the very acknowledgement of these breaches and their repair that intimate interaction can occur (Weingarten, 1992). Indeed, after I wrote this paper I offered my telling of their stories back to "Thomas," "Priscilla," "Carol," and "Mary," for repair and their revision. Each of them gave me a re-vision, a new way of seeing the story, an expanded understanding of his or her evolving relationship with God and the part our therapy and research conversations played in that evolution. And each has changed how I see God.

It is in this context of these intimate interactions that a person continues to co-create an evolving story with God that is uniquely his or her own, not dominated by my story, nor a psychological story, nor even the story of his or her particular religious doctrines. Though these other stories may compete for space in the discourse and in the mind of the therapist, and may influence and contribute to the evolving narrative, primacy must be given to that person's story as the person describes his or her experiences, with the words and the meanings the person teaches us, and the possibilities and surprises that are encountered.

My tradition says, "The Holy's other name is Surprise." If one is too certain of her specifications of God, she will miss God. A Rabbi told me that the Israelites could not wholly name God. They said "Yahweh" which meant, "I am who I am, and I will be who I will be." Movement and mystery. Still, just as I sometimes get peace confused with safety,[5] I get faith confused with certainty. I do believe though, that to search for one is to lose the other.

AUTHOR NOTE

The ideas and work offered here are the fruit of the encouragement and close collaboration with my partner, James Griffith. I am indebted in this work to many other conversational partners, Sallyann Roth, Gloria Martin, Julie Propst, and to the generosity of the persons who allowed their stories to be told here. I am especially grateful to Kathy Weingarten, not only for her thoughtful editing, but also for helping me to understand this work as resistance to cultural oppression.

NOTES

1. Our research project on Conversations with a Personal God is conducted in the Department of Psychiatry at the University of Mississippi School of Medicine. Characteristics of intrapersonal dialogues with a personal God are studied in order to learn how these dialogues can best be employed as a resource in individual and family therapies. For further information on the project, please write the author.

2. I hope these stereotyping views are not offensive. I decided to choose the Episcopalians and the Southern Baptists since I have personal affiliations with both groups and still benefit from both these associations.

3. Members of this denomination collaborated with me to construct this description.

4. Though most of the clinical and research work refers to persons who are Protestant Christians, the research team at work on the Conversations with a Personal God project includes persons who are of the Catholic, Hindu, and Greek Orthodox traditions. The members of this team have been Alexis Polles, Jeanetta Rains, Carol Tingle, Dinesh Mittal, Nancy Krejmas, James Griffith, and myself.

5. Dietrich Bonhoeffer (executed, Flossenburg Concentration Camp, 1945), pastor of the resistance to Hitler, in addressing the Christian Churches in Germany, implored them to realize that the quest for their personal safety was not the quest for peace. In fact, the actions that might insure their safety would be the very actions that would destroy God's peace, which could only come with justice.

REFERENCES

Bakhtin, M. M. (1981). *The dialogic imagination.* M. Holquist (Ed.). Austin: University of Texas Press.

Elliott-Griffith, M., & Griffith, J. L. (1992, October). Including relationships with God in therapy with religious families. Workshop presented at the 50th Annual Conference of the American Association for Marriage and Family Therapy, Miami, FL.

Gadamer, H. G. (1976). *Philosophical hermeneutics.* Berkeley: University of California Press.

Glazener, M. (1992). *The cup of wrath: The story of Dietrich Bonhoeffer's resistance to Hitler.* Savannah: Frederic C. Beil.

Griffith, J. L. (1986). Employing the God-family relationship in therapy with religious families. *Family Process, 25,* 609-618.

Griffith, J. L., Elliott-Griffith, M., Rains, J., Tingle, C., Krejmas, N., Mittal, D., & Polles, A. (1992, November). Quality of relationship between self and a personal God: Its narrative history and relationship to individual and family variables. Paper presented at the American Family Therapy Academy/George Washington University Research Conference at Captiva Island, FL.

Griffith, J. L., & Griffith, M. E. (1992). Therapeutic change in religious families–Working with the God-construct. In L. Burton (Ed.), *Religion and the family.* Binghamton, NY: The Haworth Press, Inc.

Heidegger, M. (1971). *On the way to language.* New York: Harper & Row.

Rizzuto, A. M. (1979). *The birth of the living God.* Chicago: University of Chicago Press.

Tingle, C. V., Griffith, J. L., Griffith, M. E., Rains, J., Mittal, D., & Krejmas, N. (1993, May). God-person relationships–Their character and relation to individual and family system variables. Paper presented at the 146th Annual Meeting of the American Psychiatric Association, San Francisco, CA.

Watkins, M. (1986). *Invisible guests: The development of imaginal dialogues.* Hillsdale, NJ: L. Elbaum Assoc, Inc.

Weingarten, K. (1992). A consideration of intimate and non-intimate interactions in therapy. *Family Process,* 31, 45-59.

White, M., & Epston, D. (1989). *Literate means to therapeutic ends.* Adelaide: Dulwich Centre Publications.

Response to "Opening Therapy to Conversations with a Personal God"

Sallyann Roth

I experienced Melissa Elliott Griffith's paper, "Opening Therapy to Conversations with a Personal God," as a poem, a communication aimed accurately into my heart, becoming part of me before I put a single word to my experience of reading it. Wordless, but transformed, how could I respond to it in writing? I was paralyzed. Then a woman who had taken religious vows consulted me. In the very first moments of our initial meeting, I asked her what brought her to see me. "I am here because I am an incest perpetrator and because of sexual abuse that I experienced—both many, many years ago," she said. "How is it that these things bring you here now?" I asked. She responded, "Recently I have been revisiting those scenes. I keep going back to them. I am remembering them more strongly than ever before." When she paused, I asked, "In this time that you have been revisiting those scenes so strongly, have your conversations with God changed?" She began to sob, and through her tears said, "They are less verbal and I have more of a sense of presence. And during the service I feel overwhelmed with emotion when I hear, 'Thank

---

Sallyann Roth, LICSW, is Co-Director of the Program in Narrative Therapies at the Family Institute of Cambridge in Watertown, MA.

[Haworth co-indexing entry note]: "Response to 'Opening Therapy to Conversations with a Personal God'." Roth, Sallyann. Co-published simultaneously in the *Journal of Feminist Family Therapy* (The Haworth Press, Inc.) Vol. 7, No. 1/2, 1995, pp. 141-142; and: *Cultural Resistance: Challenging Beliefs About Men, Women, and Therapy* (ed: Kathy Weingarten) The Haworth Press, Inc., 1995, pp. 141-142; and: *Cultural Resistance: Challenging Beliefs About Men, Women, and Therapy* (ed: Kathy Weingarten) Harrington Park Press, an imprint of The Haworth Press, Inc., 1995, pp. 141-142. *[Single or multiple copies of this article are available from The Haworth Document Delivery Service: 1-800-342-9678, 9:00 a.m. - 5:00 p.m. (EST).]*

© 1995 by The Haworth Press, Inc. All rights reserved.

you, God, for counting me worthy to stand in your presence and serve.' I've been able to invite God to go with me into these experiences–into my sister's bedroom as I remember my yearning, my loneliness, my terror of being found out. Now there is nothing about me that I can't bring to God." She looked up from her tears and said, "That question was a wonderful question. I was in therapy for years, and the therapist never asked anything about my conversations with God. I feel like we are right where we should be. My relationship with God is changing as I feel both better and worse, more empowered and more ashamed. All of these emotions are amplified in me . . ." I felt immediately that we were on a promising path in the work.

While Melissa works in a geographic area in which religious faith and church membership are tightly woven into the social fabric, she invites us not to ignore our clients' relationships with God even when we work in places where people are less likely to be active members of communities of faith, or where people do not speak readily about the spiritual dimension of their lives. She reminds us that in many ways when we are working with clients in relation with God, we are challenged in much the same ways that we are challenged when working with clients in relation to any "other" who is represented in the room only by the client's perceptions, meanings, and beliefs. That challenge is to honor the indeterminacy of the relationship by open-heartedly receiving that relationship into the room, by believing that it holds numerous possibilities for movement, and by conversing in a way that brings forward its many possibilities. Melissa has opened the gates of the heretofore often avoided territory of spirituality by challenging the customary reticence of secular therapists to explore clients' relationships with the numinous. Her urgings to remember that we truly don't know, cannot know, the content and generative possibilities of these relationships are as passionate as her urgings to respect their common centrality and as tender as her gentle nudge toward a serious playfulness in working with these usually intimate and infrequently revealed relationships. Any contact with another that invites me to think that which has been unthinkable, to speak that which has been unspeakable, to know that which has been unknowable, to question that which has been unquestionable, and to appreciate how much I do not–can not–know, is a gift to me. Thank you, Melissa.

From Stuck Debate
to New Conversation
on Controversial Issues:
A Report from the Public
Conversations Project

Carol Becker
Laura Chasin
Richard Chasin
Margaret Herzig
Sallyann Roth

SUMMARY. Some public controversies, such as the abortion debate, have become so chronically polarized that most citizens can-

The Public Conversations Project is an action-research project that seeks to develop models for dialogue facilitation on divisive political issues. The project was the inspiration of Laura Chasin, MSW, its founder and director. She and three other project members, Carol Becker, PhD, Richard Chasin, MD, and Sallyann Roth, MSW, are couple and family therapists and faculty members at the Family Institute of Cambridge; Margaret Herzig, the project's executive director, is a writer-researcher.

The team has been ably supported by research assistants Mary Hess (1991-1992) and Eliza Vaillant (1992-present). Our team is indebted to Kathy Weingarten for her editorial help with this article and for encouraging us to elaborate on the significance of our work for the American political process.

Written communications with the project should be sent to 2 Appleton Street, Cambridge, MA 02138.

[Haworth co-indexing entry note]: "From Stuck Debate to New Conversation on Controversial Issues: A Report from the Public Conversations Project." Becker, Carol et al. Co-published simultaneously in the *Journal of Feminist Family Therapy* (The Haworth Press, Inc.) Vol. 7, No. 1/2, 1995, pp. 143-163; and: *Cultural Resistance: Challenging Beliefs About Men, Women, and Therapy* (ed: Kathy Weingarten) The Haworth Press, Inc., 1995, pp. 143-163; and: *Cultural Resistance: Challenging Beliefs About Men, Women, and Therapy* (ed: Kathy Weingarten) Harrington Park Press, an imprint of The Haworth Press, Inc., 1995, pp. 143-163. [Single or multiple copies of this article are available from The Haworth Document Delivery Service: 1-800-342-9678, 9:00 a.m. - 5:00 p.m. (EST).]

© 1995 by The Haworth Press, Inc. All rights reserved.

not even think about them without falling into the adversarial discourse of the embattled movement leaders. The authors, who comprise the Public Conversations Project, use family systems ideas to design and conduct dialogue sessions where people with opposing views resist the pull of polarization and instead speak from the heart about personal experiences, express doubts, and show respectful curiosity with people whom they may previously have regarded as stupid, malevolent or hopelessly wrong-minded. *[Single or multiple copies of this article are available from The Haworth Document Delivery Service: 1-800-342-9678, 9:00 a.m. - 5:00 p.m. (EST).]*

When democracy works well, an emerging political problem stimulates broad and open public discussion. Concerned individuals and groups analyze the dilemma and a wide range of advocates submit carefully argued positions for public deliberation. Political leaders propose policy solutions. Ultimately, a majority of the people or their representatives construct a resolution that is acceptable or at least tolerable to everyone.

Many public controversies are resolved through some sequence of problem definition, analysis, advocacy, argument, discussion, compromise, and resolution. However, political disputes do not always follow such a course. Some controversies become defined by opposing views that cluster around two seemingly irreconcilable poles. In these instances, democratic procedures often become perversely counter-productive. Analysis becomes a slave to dogma; advocacy gets laced with vituperation; argument degenerates into diatribe; and discussions deteriorate into shouting matches. Thus every aspect of the public debate is hamstrung by polemics. Compromise is broadly seen as surrender and a widely acceptable resolution becomes hard to imagine. Once disputes become this divisive, the time-honored practices of democracy seem only to intensify and entrench the conflict.

The Public Conversations Project seeks to understand such deadlocks, and more important, to discover and experiment with forms of public discussion that might release hot controversies from polarized public debate so that democratic resolution can become possible. We have been especially interested in what happens to people when they engage in or witness conversations on polarized public issues. How do they speak and listen? What parts of themselves do they open or shut down?

THE DOMINANT DISCOURSE
IN POLARIZED PUBLIC DEBATE

Polarized public conversations can be described as conforming to a "dominant discourse." The dominant discourse is the most generally available and accepted way of discussing the issue in a public context. For example, the dominant discourse about the American Revolutionary War defined the war as one of colonial liberation. It is not usually described in the United States as a conspiracy of tax dodgers led by a multi-millionaire from Virginia.

Dominant discourses strongly influence which ideas, experiences, and observations are regarded as normal or eccentric, relevant or irrelevant.[1] On a subject that has been hotly polarized for a long time, the dominant discourse often delineates the issue in a win-lose bi-polar way; it draws a line between two simple answers to a complex dilemma and induces people to take a stand on one side of that line or the other. (For example, you are either a royalist or a revolutionary.) Most people who care deeply about the issue yield to this induction.

Being aligned with one group offers benefits. It gives one a socially validated place to stand while speaking and it offers the unswerving support of like-minded people.[2] It also exacts costs. It portrays opponents as a single-minded and malevolent gang. In the face of such frightening and unified adversaries, one's own group must be unified, strong, and certain. To be loyal to that group, one must suppress many uncertainties, morally complicated personal experiences, inner value conflicts, and differences between oneself and one's allies. Complexity and authenticity are sacrificed to the demands of presenting a unified front to the opponent. A dominant discourse of antagonism is self-perpetuating. Win-lose exchanges create losers who feel they must retaliate to regain lost respect, integrity, and security, and winners who fear to lose disputed territory won at great cost.[3,4]

The dominant discourse on polarized issues is fostered and sustained by a number of forces, most obviously, the media. The drama of polarized debate seems to capture the public's interest more than stories of subtle shifts in understanding on complicated issues. As simplified and dramatic conflicts about a controversial issue become more and more accepted by the public and the media, more complicated viewpoints seem less and less to the point, as if they are not about the issue at all.

Polarized public debates exact costs not only from those who directly participate in them, but also from those who do not. Those who are conflicted or uncertain may come to believe that their views are unwelcome in public discussions. Those who are aware of discordance between some of their personal beliefs and the political position espoused by "like-minded" others may choose to place themselves safely on the sidelines. They may worry that if they speak about their reluctance to become politically active on one side of the battle line they will be viewed as soft, muddled, unprincipled, or even as traitors. They may stop conversing even with themselves, assuming that if there is no societal validation for their views or the experiences that have shaped their views, then their views and experiences must be worthless, dangerous, or aberrant. The political process is deprived of their voices and their ideas and democracy suffers.[5]

DIALOGUE AS AN ALTERNATIVE TO POLARIZED DEBATE

Dialogue, as we use the term, involves an exchange of perspectives, experiences, and beliefs in which people speak and listen openly and respectfully. In political debates, people speak from a position of certainty, defending their own beliefs, challenging and attacking the other side, and attempting to persuade others to their point of view.[6] They generally speak not as individuals, but as representatives of a position defined by the dominant discourse. In dialogue, participants speak as unique individuals about their own beliefs and experiences, reveal their uncertainties as well as certainties, and try to understand one another.[7] As people in dialogue listen openly and respectfully to each other, their relationship shifts from one of opposition to one of interest–and sometimes to one of compassion and even empathic connection. The limitations of the dominant discourse are often acknowledged and possibilities for moving beyond it may be considered. Differences among participants become less frightening and may even begin to look more like potential social resources than insurmountable social problems. Old patterns of retaliation lose their appeal as the experience of dialogue leaves people feeling listened to and respected rather than beaten and embittered, or victorious and braced for backlash.

BRINGING CLINICAL SKILLS TO WORK ON DIALOGUE

Why did a group of family therapists enter the arena of divisive public issues? We were not certain at the outset that we had anything at all to offer in the realm of "public conversations." Our hopefulness was grounded in our observations of similarities between polarized public conversations and "stuck" family conversations. In conflicted couples and families, each person overgeneralizes and builds a case about the other person. That case is supported by selective perception of confirming data and inattention to exceptions, ambiguity and alternative ideas. In conversations replete with blaming and counter-attack, one hears self-fulfilling prophecies that fuel the futile and seemingly endless conflict.

In our consulting rooms we see families and couples move from impasse to dialogue–from closed to more open conversations.[8] We see that relationships characterized by anger and fear, and relationships of domination and subordination, can be transformed and that people with different experiences and ideas can find ways of being together that do not require either self-silencing or shouting. We hoped to use our clinical skills to create conditions in which partisans trapped in frozen patterns of speaking could shape new ways of talking and listening, in which they could participate fully as complex individuals.

We chose the abortion controversy as the focus of our early efforts in dialogue facilitation. We wondered what would happen if we offered partisans with strong views on abortion an opportunity to experience their differences in a safe atmosphere, one where inner conflicts and ethically perplexing personal experiences would be welcome and urges to convert the other side to the "correct" way of thinking would be set aside.[9] If we offered them the same sense of safety and respect that we offer our clients, could they speak about the issue and their differences in a way that differed from the predictable accounts favored by the dominant discourse? If so, what previously silent voices might be heard? How would differences and similarities within and across groups be encountered? Through dialogue, could full participation in a group that welcomed diversity come to be valued as much as, or more than, the security of belonging to one "like-minded" side or the other? If, in such a group, conversation were released from the dams of political correctness, could the free flow of genuine exploration deposit fertile soil for the growth of new ideas and relationships?[10]

BACKGROUND ON THE MODEL

The project team has worked together intensively on this project since 1989.[11] Our goal has been to develop and disseminate models that are relatively easy to use so that people who have facilitation skills can conduct dialogue sessions on public issues without having to go through the demanding process of developing models themselves.

The model that we have most fully tested is for a single dialogue session among strangers who have different views on abortion.[12] We have conducted 19 dialogue sessions with prochoice and prolife participants. Most participant groups ranged in size from four to eight people and were evenly balanced with people who described themselves as prochoice or prolife. We found that groups of six were ideal because they were large enough to offer variety and small enough to allow all to speak and get to know each other as individuals in the time available. We convened mixed gender and single gender groups. Most sessions took place from 6:00 to 9:30 p.m. on weekday evenings at the Family Institute of Cambridge in Watertown, MA.

Some of our dialogue participants were activists with local organizations (e.g., Mass Choice and Massachusetts Citizens for Life). Some participants were not politically active on the issue of abortion, but all clearly identified themselves as being either prochoice or prolife. Our early groups were primarily white, educated, and middle class; later groups included people of more diverse educational, racial, ethnic and economic backgrounds.

Two sessions were held with only two participants. One of these involved two public spokespeople on abortion who asked us to facilitate a dialogue between them. The other was a dialogue that we initiated with two graduate students in Cambridge who, as undergraduates three years earlier, had been student leaders on opposing sides of a highly publicized campus battle about abortion. Two evening sessions were held in Jackson, Mississippi, one with a women's group, and one with women in a church group. These sessions were co-facilitated by Sallyann Roth, from our project, and Melissa Griffith, a family therapist in Jackson. We designed and facilitated a full-day session for a group of eighteen women in a small town in Pennsylvania whose community was heatedly divided over abortion.

Before discussing our genèral principles and methods, we will outline the basic steps in our current one-session model.[13] We report here only on that model because we have tested it more fully than the adaptations we have developed during the past year.

OUTLINE OF THE MODEL

In our initial telephone call with participants, we take whatever time is needed to describe our process and goals, to answer questions, and to respond to any reservations that a potential participant may express. In the letter, which includes a copy of our dialogue-debate table (see Table 1), we reiterate our goals and outline some of the agreements we propose to foster a safe atmosphere during the dialogue. We also give participants some questions to ponder and explicitly request that they bring to the dialogue session "the part of you that listens thoughtfully and respectfully to others, not the part that is prone to persuade, defend or attack."

When participants arrive, we share with them a light buffet dinner during which they get acquainted with each other and with us. Each person takes a couple of minutes to say something about him or her self. Participants are asked not to include information that would indicate where they stand on the issue. After dinner, but before going to the interview room, participants sign video releases that they can rescind later.

We begin the session by proposing that participants make agreements with each other to maintain confidentiality; to use respectful language (e.g., "prolife" and "prochoice," not "anti-choice" and "anti-abortion"); to let each person finish speaking (i.e., no interrupting); and to allow each other to decline to answer any question

TABLE 1. Distinguishing Debate from Dialogue*

DEBATE	DIALOGUE
Pre-meeting communication between sponsors and participants is minimal and largely irrelevant to what follows.	Pre-meeting contacts and preparation of participants are essential elements of the full process.
Participants tend to be leaders known for propounding a carefully crafted position. The personas displayed in the debate are usually already familiar to the public. The behavior of the participants tends to conform to stereotypes.	Those chosen to participate are not necessarily outspoken "leaders." Whoever they are, they speak as individuals whose own unique experiences differ in some respect from others on their "side." Their behavior is likely to vary in some degree and along some dimensions from stereotypic images others may hold of them.
The atmosphere is threatening; attacks and interruptions are expected by participants and are usually permitted by moderators.	The atmosphere is one of safety; facilitators propose, get agreement on, and enforce clear ground rules to enhance safety and promote respectful exchange.
Participants speak as representatives of groups.	Participants speak as individuals, from their own unique experience.
Participants speak to their own constituents and, perhaps, to the undecided middle.	Participants speak to each other.
Differences within the "sides" are denied or minimized.	Differences among participants on the same "side" are revealed, as individual and personal foundations of beliefs and values are explored.
Participants express unswerving commitment to a point of view, approach, or idea.	Participants express uncertainties, as well as deeply held beliefs.
Participants listen in order to refute the other side's data and to expose faulty logic in their arguments. Questions are asked from a position of certainty. These questions are often rhetorical challenges or disguised statements.	Participants listen to understand and gain insight into the beliefs and concerns of the others. Questions are asked from a position of curiosity.
Statements are predictable and offer little new information.	New information surfaces.
Success requires simple impassioned statements.	Success requires exploration of the complexities of the issue being discussed.
Debates operate within the constraints of the dominant public discourse. (The discourse defines the problem and the options for resolution. It assumes that fundamental needs and values are already clearly understood.)	Participants are encouraged to question the dominant public discourse, that is, to express fundamental needs that may or may not be reflected in the discourse and to explore various options for problem definition and resolution. Participants may discover inadequacies in the usual language and concepts used in the public debate.

* This table contrasts debate as commonly seen on television with the kind of dialogue we aim to promote in dialogue sessions conducted by the Public Conversations Project.
© The Public Conversations Project of the Family Institute of Cambridge, 51 Kondazian Street, Watertown, MA 02172.

without needing to explain (i.e., participants have the "right to pass").[14] The facilitators outline the schedule for the evening and remind participants that they "have an opportunity here to have a different conversation, one in which you will be able to share your thoughts and feelings and what you struggle with . . . This is a time to speak as unique individuals and be with people with different views and ask questions about which you are genuinely curious." Participants are also reminded to set aside the urge to persuade.

During the first 45 minutes of the session, the facilitators ask three questions of the participants. The first two questions are answered in "go-rounds," that is, each participant answers the same question in turn. The third is answered "popcorn-style," i.e., the speaking sequence is determined by readiness to speak, not by seating arrangement.

After the participants have responded to our opening questions, we invite them to ask questions of each other. Before they start, we suggest that these questions be ones that arise from their genuine curiosity about each other, and not be rhetorical questions or statements in disguise. We remind them that this is not a time to persuade, and we suggest that they speak about themselves and ask questions about each other (not about "they" and "them" outside of the room).

About twenty minutes before the session is scheduled to end, we ask: "What do you think you have done or not done to make this conversation go as it has?" and "Do you have any parting thoughts that you'd like to share?" At the end, we ask participants if they would like to alter the agreements they made about confidentiality and about allowing us to keep the video of the session for research purposes. We also ask permission to call them for feedback.

A few weeks after the session, we call participants to elicit feedback as a guide to improving the model, to ask about their further thoughts, and to learn what they have taken or might yet take from the session into their lives. Follow-up calls usually last about 45 minutes. Most are taped and transcribed.

GUIDING OBJECTIVES

The principles guiding our work are closely tied to each other and interwoven in each step in the model. In this paper we will somewhat artificially tease out four general objectives and indicate what principles they reflect and what methods they guide. The four objectives are: (1) preparing participants for a journey into the new; (2) creating a safe context; (3) avoiding the old debate; and (4) fostering the co-creation of a new conversation.

PREPARING PARTICIPANTS FOR A JOURNEY INTO THE NEW

In our initial phone call with participants, in the letter of invitation, and in our orienting remarks at the beginning of the session, we clearly distinguish between *dialogue,* as we understand it, and *debate* as typically seen on television (see Table 1). We aim to leave no room for misunderstanding about the nature of the event, as we want people to participate with informed consent. We want those who feel unwilling to set aside the urge to persuade, or who are uninterested in respectful exploratory exchanges with the "other side," to self-select out of the process. (Only four people, two on each "side," have declined participation for such reasons).

There is a second reason for our fully presenting our thinking to participants. Although our structured process is totally voluntary, participants can experience it as so unnatural and anxiety provoking that they may seek refuge in the familiar. To help participants resist this retreat, we highlight the differences between the usual discourse on abortion and a new dialogue among individuals to prepare them for the challenges of their voyage into the new.

We prepare them in many ways. We outline our expectations for their session, spell out specific agreements we will propose to ensure their safety throughout the session, and indicate what they might ponder in getting ready for it. We also hold before them the image of an achievable alternative to divisive debate when we mention that past participants have been able to participate with integrity and respectful curiosity, and speak about their own views and experiences with authenticity.[15]

The careful and patient way we convey this information to participants models the respectfulness and attentiveness that will be expected of them in the dialogue. Our early interactions with participants give them reason to believe that we will diligently assist them in maintaining their agreements and consistently support the part of them that is open to listening respectfully, speaking in new ways, and learning something new about others and about themselves.

CREATING A SAFE CONTEXT

People are unlikely to risk openness with adversaries unless they are assured of safety. If we ask participants to come rhetorically disarmed then we must provide protection. We believe that the extensive care with which we prepare participants for the event contributes to their sense of safety. The more they know about it the safer they feel. What they learn about our approach also helps. They discover immediately that we provide explicit expectations and a definite structure for the session; they need not worry about encountering adversaries in a free-for-all setting. They learn that we ask for specific agreements that effectively reduce any fears they might have of public exposure, rude interruptions, hurtful insults, and pressure to speak against their will.

Another way in which we foster safety is through role clarity regarding process and content. As facilitators, we provide a structure and facilitate a process; we do not contribute on the level of content. We ask for and earn the participants' trust that we will dedicate our energy to their safety as they explore experience and meaning with themselves and each other.

The participants' feeling of safety is also supported by the respectful way in which we involve them in our process of learning. We approach them not as "subjects," but as co-investigators. We present ourselves not as all-knowing experts prepared to judge them but as explorers interested in their guidance. In follow-up calls we ask participants about every phase of the process. We ask what helped and what hindered their journey. If participants report uncomfortable moments, we ask if they have ideas as to how we might have helped them at that moment, or reduced their discomfort. Follow-up calls represent opportunities for us not only to learn, but to demonstrate our continued interest in participants' safety, integrity and well-being.

AVOIDING THE OLD DEBATE

Several features of our model constitute interventions designed to prevent the old conversation and make room for a new one. When we ask people not to reveal where they stand on the issue during dinner, we prevent participants from sizing each other up through the lenses of friend or foe. This allows them to meet as unique individuals. They sometimes make guesses about who will be on which side, and find that they are not always correct. This gives them an opportunity to notice their own stereotyping process at work.

When participants enter the dialogue room they are assigned seats next to rather than opposite people with different views. This breaks up the usual face-off of opposing sides and leads to a sequence of responses in the opening go-rounds that highlights variety and interrupts tendencies to group people into "camps."

The agreements and guidelines that we propose avoid fruitless and destructive patterns of interaction. The pass rule frees people to make inquiries and it protects everyone from being cornered. The go-round structure and the agreement about not interrupting prevent reactivity and help listeners to set aside habits of preparing responses while others are speaking. Guidelines about speaking personally, avoiding rhetorical questions, and leaving "they" and "them" out of the room block polemics, grandstanding and blaming.

In parting comments and follow-up calls, participants sometimes comment on the liberating effect of these constraints. One man said, "Taking the superheat out of it at least allows you to hear the other point of view better . . . [It] provides an opportunity to be a little more of who you are and a little less guarded." Another man said that the safety offered through the ground rules allowed him to share his uncertainties. He said, "If I were debating this issue I wouldn't have told you half these things." One woman commented at the end of her session that it was "a personal victory" that she did not feel a need to make a closing comment "meant to persuade." Another said that she is usually vulnerable to "group think" but in this case "she really felt everything she said." A few people have said that they noticed themselves biting their tongues. One man, in his closing remarks during the session, said that he didn't feel totally honest setting aside strong language. However, in his follow-up call, he described the tone of the exchange as "admirable" and he commended the facilitators for "keeping the thing on track" without making anyone feel "hamstrung or crowded." When he was asked about his parting comment during the session, he said that it had been good for him to shape his comments with our guidelines in mind. "Let's face it," he said, "arguments are a dime a dozen. This was unique."[16]

FOSTERING CO-CREATION
OF A NEW CONVERSATION

We begin the process of encouraging a new conversation when we propose and reiterate the "alternative frame," i.e., when we set goals and offer guidelines for a conversation that differs fundamentally from debate.[17] We establish a tone that is heartfelt, curious, open and respectful. We set a slow pace. By the time the floor is turned over to participants, they clearly understand how we view the old "stuck" conversation and what elements we expect may emerge in a new one: curiosity, complexity, personal narrative, and sharing of uncertainties as well as certainties. The opening questions are carefully worded and sequenced to encourage these elements. They are designed with the recognition that chronic political conflict is generally not amenable to resolution through discussions of facts; it is generally rooted in deeply personal experiences and values.

The first question is: *We would like you to say something about your own life experiences in relation to the issue of abortion. For example, something about your personal history with the issue, how you got interested in it, what your involvement has been.* This question grounds the discussion in rich personal narratives and reveals connections between strongly held beliefs and subjective experiences. For some participants, it leads to reflections on the beliefs that were "in the air" in their families. For some it elicits poignant stories about abortions, adoptions, tragedies, triumphs and complicated turns of events in the lives of individuals and families. Interest is high and curiosity is stirred; no story is predictable.

Prolife Woman: As a sophomore, my closest friend took it upon herself to be president of the prolife group on campus . . . [She] was physically handicapped with cerebral palsy and she was very concerned about the value our society places on handicapped individuals. She died, for reasons we still don't understand to this day, and I couldn't bear to see all that she worked so hard for go by the wayside. . . . At this point, I had come to what I term a prolife feminist position.

Prochoice Man: Well, I was catapulted into this many decades ago because my sister had an abortion and it turned out that the baby's father was my father. And that's a hard place to begin to think about all this stuff. When I was married, my wife had three miscarriages before our son was born and I have seen what it does to a woman, even in terms of that being something she has no control over. . . . I cannot advise people about [abortion]. I have to see what their particular feeling is.

The second question, *What's at the heart of the matter for you as an individual?* gives people an opportunity to say what they need to say about their convictions but it locates the core of the issue in the heartfelt, the unique and the personal. Throughout the session, our language draws participants' attention to what they care most about.

Prochoice Woman: I think the moral maturity of women is what's really at stake for me. Anything that legislates or removes choice from an individual woman removes the respect for her as a mature, moral person who is capable of making decisions that are right for her in the context of her life and her relationships.

Prolife Woman: The fact that a child is wanted or not wanted by someone else–it would frighten me to think that the importance of my life is contingent upon the fact that someone wants me. I am special in myself and it doesn't matter to me whether someone wants me. My life certainly shouldn't depend on it at any stage.

We pose the third question as follows: *Many people have within their general approach to abortion some gray areas, some dilem-*

mas about their own beliefs, or even some conflicts within themselves. Sometimes these gray areas are revealed when people consider hard cases–circumstances in which a prolife person might want to allow an abortion, or situations in which a prochoice person might not want to permit an abortion. Or, in a very different way, sometimes an individual feels that his or her own views on abortion come into conflict with other important values and beliefs. We have found it to be productive and helpful when people share whatever dilemmas, struggles, and conflicts they have within their prevailing view. We invite you to mention any pockets of uncertainty or lesser certainty, any concerns, value conflicts, or mixed feelings you may have and wish to share. This question brings forth differentiation among the views of those with similar positions and suggests bridges between those on different sides. It encourages participants to grapple with the complexity of their own views.

> *Prolife Man:* I guess the way I look at it, if you terminate that life . . . there's an evil there. If it's a case of an unwanted pregnancy, there's an evil there. If it's a byproduct of rape or incest, if you have a severely impaired baby in the process, all of those things are evils. And where the uncertainty comes in for me is [in a situation like] a 13 year old girl has just been raped by her uncle and it's basically going to destroy her life. . . . And I can't just sit there and say, on my high moral horse, "It's the ultimate universal wrong to kill an unborn child." Because I know that there are other bad things in the world and you've got to balance them.

> *Prochoice Woman:* The sanctity of life is precious to me . . . and I don't think God takes it lightly that we make a decision about choosing to end a life, for whatever reason it may be. I would like us not to make abortion something we can do without having to think about it. . . . I don't think there is a right answer. Sometimes there is a less bad answer than another.

> *Prolife Woman:* One time I was discussing this issue with a friend and he said, "Obviously you never grew up an unwanted child." And he was right, they wanted me. I think of the children that suffer and think to myself, would it have been better if they had been aborted? Then I think, well, they have

life. But it's really hard to watch children in pain and sometimes it's hard to be prolife, but I'm so prolife. So that's something I really struggle with.

Prochoice Woman: After I had my baby I realized that I would
never have an abortion, personally. That changed my personal
view of abortion. . . . It bothers me that there hasn't been much
dialogue within the prochoice community about how far along
abortions should be allowed. To me an end point would be 5 or
6 months. That, to me, is the point where we are talking about
a baby, not a fetus.

Some prolife participants have said that their moral position
about abortion conflicts with their political belief in a pluralistic
society founded on the idea that different values can co-exist. A
prochoice woman said that thoughts about the damage done to
children by drugs and alcohol before they are born are what evoke
in her compassion for the fetus. This is when she entertains the idea
that the fetus may have rights. A feminist prolife woman explained
her belief that legal abortions allow women to be used by men who
do not have to take responsibility for their actions; abortion
becomes a substitute for finding solutions to the social problems of
our time. She said that a woman's choice is not a genuine choice
until it is made in the context of equally viable alternatives. She
indicated that she is ambivalent about prohibiting abortions in a
society without adequate supports for women facing unplanned
pregnancies.

During the time in which we call for questions of curiosity, we
have witnessed many meaningful and interesting exchanges. A prochoice leader asked a prolife leader if he could think of any reasons
for keeping abortion legal. He said that he could: women would not
die from illegal abortions. A Jewish prochoice woman asked a
Catholic prolife woman active in Operation Rescue to describe her
views about the relationship between abortion and the soul. The
prolife woman disclosed a complex belief system about what happens to the soul of an aborted baby.

Hearing about beliefs in a more complex manner than can be
conveyed through slogans, hearing about ambiguities usually suppressed, and finding and revealing one's own silenced complexities

and dilemmas can be both humbling and empowering. At the end of one session, one woman said, "None of us knows the truth. But together we can come closer to the truth. We can be safe, liberated and accepted. We can continue struggling, even though we may never have it right." Sometimes the experience of listening and speaking in a new way in the dialogue group contains lessons for participants' personal relationships. One woman said, "I'm afraid I really don't make room for others' views if they are different from mine. I don't make room for my husband's views. I don't like that about myself. I want to change that." Another woman commented that it is hard to share personal experiences with people who hold opposing ideological positions, "but this is, in my mind how human community is formed and deepens. We do not change the world by staying on two sides of the fence and yelling at each other."

DIALOGUE IN DEMOCRACY

Democratic governments guarantee free speech to foster full participation in public life by all citizens. However, as we have discussed, sometimes sociopolitical forces within a democracy create a dominant discourse on a polarized issue that discourages citizens from speaking fully on that issue. Some people with complicated views silence themselves entirely. As a result, complex human and social dilemmas turn into bitter polarized stand-offs that drain precious resources into a pool of hopelessness and hatred.

A major goal of our project is to create a replicable process in which citizens can enjoy full, safe and respectful dialogues on controversial issues. If we and others with facilitation skills can create and foster such a process, then the grip of the dominant discourse on polarized issues can be loosened and previously silenced voices can be heard in more public conversations. To the extent that more members of society are included in a forum and all who enter that forum include more of themselves in it, we believe that the spirit of democracy will be served.

Each of us joined the project with somewhat different perspectives and experiences pertaining to the abortion debate, but all of us have come to appreciate how much our thinking had been constrained by the dominant discourse on abortion and the stereotypes it fosters. Witnessing and facilitating these conversations has been a source of humility and excitement. It has deepened our commitment to the project's objectives. Our experiences have reinforced our belief that the rhetoric of the abortion controversy has belittled valid concerns, denigrated positive social values, and obscured rich and complex meanings. We are increasingly certain that dialogue is essential to the democratic society, to keep it alive in spirit and practice as well as in law, to keep it responsive to its diverse participants, and inclusive of all who live their lives within it. We count among our own ways of participating in democracy our work on this project and we are delighted to have the opportunity to share this work with our colleagues in this journal.

NOTES

1. Thus, discourses have the power to amplify and validate some experiences and to dismiss and invalidate others. Our work shares with feminist family therapy the goal of questioning oppressive discourses (whether they are bipolar or hierarchical) and encouraging full participation of all those whose voices have been marginalized by them.

2. See John Mack (1983, 1988) on the psychological mechanisms by which political loyalties and relations of enmity form.

3. Social psychologist Herbert Kelman, who has developed problem-solving workshops for Israelis and Palestinians, has found that analyses of chronic political conflict usually reveal fundamental threats to identity, security, and acceptance (Kelman, 1990, p. 156).

4. In a voluntary community like a church, polarized win-lose debates may lead some members to leave. The Mennonites have developed a "conciliation service" to help church groups address issues that "stir strong feelings" (Buxman, 1992).

5. As described by Shotter (1992), some polarized debates are embedded in political struggles of identity in which marginalized groups seek a sense of belonging in a community in which a favored "situational knowledge" has prevailed.

6. Polarized debate, at its worst, has been referred to as "reciprocated diatribe" (Freeman, Littlejohn, & Pearce 1992).

7. Although increased understanding is one goal of dialogue, we do not intend to portray dialogue as a linear movement from incomplete to complete understanding. As Gurevitch (1988, 1989) argues, dialogue often involves the debunking of the way we "understand" the other within our own reality, recognition that we don't and can't fully understand the other, and acknowledgment of "the existence of more than one authoritative origin of meaning, truth, and justice" (1989, p. 171). See also Roth (1992).

8. For a more detailed discussion of "therapeutic conversations," see Anderson and Goolishian (1988).

9. On moving beyond "the urge to persuade," see White (1986/87).

10. In his book The Magic of Conflict, *aikido* instructor Thomas Crum describes such a release as moving from "a point of view to a viewing point–a higher, more expansive place from which you can see both sides," p. 166.

11. In our early months of brainstorming, our team included two other colleagues from the Family Institute of Cambridge, Kathy Weingarten and Terry Real, and television writer/producer, Peter Cook from WGBH-TV, Boston.

12. We have begun to experiment with various adaptations of that model for use on other topics, in varied settings, and with different kinds of participant groups. For example, we have designed two one-day meetings and one three-day meeting for US social policy activists concerned with population and women's health. These activists had many common concerns and goals but they tended not to cooperate with each other because they had historical grievances with each other and different priorities that they perceived as incompatible. We have also consulted to individuals who work to foster dialogue on gay rights and rent control. Laura Chasin and Caroline Marvin worked with a women's church organization concerned about conflicts in their diocese over race and homosexuality. We conducted a day-long session with a civic group that had been actively embattled over abortion for two years. Sallyann Roth designed and implemented a day-long workshop for a mental health agency experiencing tensions between gay and straight staff (Roth, 1992). Margaret Herzig worked with Grady McGonagill, and two other organizational consultants, to co-facilitate a two-day dialogue retreat with environmentalists, timber industry representatives, and property rights advocates in "The Northern Forest."

13. For more detailed information about various steps in the model, see Becker et al., 1992, Chasin and Herzig, 1993, and Roth et al., 1992.

14. The "pass rule" was originated by James Sacks and described by Lee (1981), Chasin, Roth, and Bograd (1989), and Roth and Chasin (1994).

15. In this way, we contrast the constraining influence of the dominant discourse with what is possible when one resists this influence in favor of speaking fully. In Michael White's terms, we "externalize the problem" (White, 1989).

16. When we speak of dialogue as fostering a sense of integrity and authenticity, we do not mean to suggest that expressions of strong belief have no place in "authentic" expression. In dialogue facilitation we see ourselves as dedicating the session to making room for ideas and feelings that are usually suppressed. In a social system characterized by oppressively bland homogeneity, encouraging suppressed voices would also involve blocking "old" patterns, but those patterns would be different, e.g., they would be characterized by politeness and deference rather than animosity and vitriol. In either case, encouraging people to speak as individuals from their personal experience is likely to give voice to what is usually unspoken and to give a less polarizing tone to strongly held beliefs.

17. See Anderson and Goolishian (1988) on "co-creating" a new conversation.

REFERENCES

Anderson, H. & H. Goolishian (1988). Humans systems as linguistic systems: Some preliminary and evolving ideas about the implications for clinical theory. *Family Process,* 27:4, 371-393.

Buxman, B. (1992). Working through conflict: A testimony. *MCS Conciliation Quarterly,* 11:1, p. 4.

Chasin, L. (unpublished). Population and family planning in context: Steps toward a shared vision: A report on a dialogue weekend at Chappaquiddick.

Chasin, L., R. Chasin, M. Herzig, S. Roth & C. Becker (1991). The citizen clinician: The family therapist in the public forum. *American Family Therapy Association Newsletter,* Winter, 36-42.

Chasin, R. & M. Herzig (1993). Creating systemic interventions for the sociopolitical arena. In B. Berger-Gould & D. H. DeMuth (Eds.), *The global family therapist: Integrating the personal, professional and political.* Needham, Mass., U.S.A.: Allyn and Bacon, 141-192.

Chasin, R., S. Roth & M. Bograd (1989). Action methods in systemic therapy: Dramatizing ideal futures and reformed pasts with couples. *Family Process,* 28, 121-136.

Crum, T. (1987). *The magic of conflict.* Aiki Works, Inc., PO Box 7845, Aspen, CO 81612.

Freeman, Sally A., Stephen W. Littlejohn, & W. B. Pearce (1992). Communication and moral conflict. *Western Journal of Communication,* 56, 311-329.

Gurevitch, Z.D. (1988). The other side of dialogue: On making the other strange and the experience of otherness. *American Journal of Sociology,* 93, 1179-1199.

Gurevitch, Z.D. (1989). The power of not understanding: The meeting of conflicting identities. *The Journal of Applied Behavioral Science,* 25, 161-173.

Kelman, Herbert (1990). Interactive problem solving: The uses and limits of a therapeutic model for the resolution of international conflicts. In Volkan, Montville, & Julius, (Eds.), *The psychodynamics of international relationships.* Lexington, Mass.: Lexington Books.

Lee, R. (1981). Video as adjunct to psychodrama and role-playing. In J. Fryrear & R. Fleshman (Eds.), *Videotherapy and mental health.* Springfield, Ill: Charles C Thomas.

Mack, J. (1983). Nationalism and the self. *The Psychohistory Review,* 11:2/3, 47-69.

Mack, J. (1988). The enemy system. *The Lancet.* August 13, 385-387.

Roth, S. (1992). Speaking the unspoken: A work-group consultation to reopen dialogue. In E. Imber-Black (Ed.), *Secrets in families and family therapy.* New York: Norton, 268-291.

Roth, S., L. Chasin, R. Chasin, C. Becker & M. Herzig (1992). From debate to dialogue: A facilitating role for family therapists in the public forum. *Dulwich Centre Newsletter,* No. 2, 41-48.

Roth, S. & R. Chasin (in press). Entering One Another's Worlds of Meaning and

Imagination. In *Dramatic enactment and narrative couple therapy.* New York: Guilford.

Shotter, J. (1992). Bakhtin and Billig: Monological versus dialogical practices. *American Behavioral Scientist,* 36:1, 8-12.

White, M. (1986/87). Couple therapy: "Urging for sameness" or "appreciation of difference." *Dulwich Centre Newsletter,* Summer, 11-13.

White, M. (1989). The externalizing of the problem and the re-authoring of lives and relationships. *Dulwich Centre Newsletter.* Summer, 3-21.

Commentary
on "From Stuck Debate
to New Conversation
on Controversial Issues:
A Report from the Public
Conversations Project"

Michael White

Human beings are surely interpreting beings. From infancy, we strive to give meaning to our experiences of the world. For all of us, this "meaning making" project is a complex one; and it is for life. We are perpetually engaged in the negotiation of a multiplicity of possible meanings, many of which are mutually contradictory.

This project requires that we work hard to resolve the dilemmas posed by the array of competing meanings that confront us as we move through the different sites of culture that we inhabit—work, school, leisure, etc. Since this negotiation of meaning occurs within the context of communities of people, it is all the more complex and problematic. These processes are characterized by a contestation of "facts" and by argument. On this account, meaning-making engages us in struggles of both intrapersonal and interpersonal kinds.

Michael White is Co-Director of Dulwich Centre in Adelaide, South Australia. His work is partly informed by the narrative metaphor and by attention to the politics of peoples' experience.

[Haworth co-indexing entry note]: "Commentary on 'From Stuck Debate to New Conversation on Controversial Issues: A Report from the Public Conversations Project'." White, Michael. Co-published simultaneously in the *Journal of Feminist Family Therapy* (The Haworth Press, Inc.) Vol. 7, No. 1/2, 1995, pp. 165-167; and: *Cultural Resistance: Challenging Beliefs About Men, Women, and Therapy* (ed: Kathy Weingarten) The Haworth Press, Inc., 1995, pp. 165-167; and: *Cultural Resistance: Challenging Beliefs About Men, Women, and Therapy* (ed: Kathy Weingarten) Harrington Park Press, an imprint of The Haworth Press, Inc., 1995, pp. 165-167. *[Single or multiple copies of this article are available from The Haworth Document Delivery Service: 1-800-342-9678, 9:00 a.m. - 5:00 p.m. (EST).]*

© 1995 by The Haworth Press, Inc. All rights reserved.

It is when this struggle becomes routinized, formalized and polarized that it captures people. When this happens, contestation and argumentation at the intrapersonal and interpersonal levels is virtually eliminated. Meaning-making becomes frozen in time and people on both sides of the divide experience the threat of domination.

This phenomenon is evident in the form of those modern adversarial practices that occur in most sites of culture: in families, in universities, in courtrooms, in the institutions of micro and macro politics, and so on. These adversarial practices are characterized by "impressive" ways of speaking and by specific techniques of power.

Impressive ways of speaking are disembodied ways of speaking. They are utilized to establish claims to objective knowledge and to certainty by:

1. obscuring the personal motives or the conscious purposes of the speaker.
2. erasing all information about the personal experiences that provide the context for the generation of these knowledge claims.
3. excluding all details about the intra and interpersonal struggle that is associated with the process of meaning-making; processes that are characterized by dilemmas, by contention and by argument.
4. diverting attention from those personal investments that are informed by peoples' location in the social worlds of gender, culture, race, ethnicity, class, sexual preference, and so on.
5. deleting all reference to the history of controversy that surrounds all claims to objective knowledge.

The techniques of power associated with these adversarial practices, a number of which are spelled out by the authors, are designed to discourage resistance and to silence protest. These techniques serve to objectify and marginalize others, to degrade and to disqualify their voices.

Against the backdrop of the pervasiveness of these adversarial practices, practices which structure so many of our relations to each other, the work of Becker et al. is significant. They have made it their business to develop contexts that make it possible for people to break their lives from these adversarial practices; to challenge the formalization of debate; to redeem argument; and to honor the contestatory nature of "facts."

Their proposal for public conversation includes prologues, ground rules and interactive tasks that are informed by an alternative ethic. This ethic is not mired in the imperatives of control, consensus, or agreement. Theirs is a proposal for a structure that establishes a space that is relatively free of the techniques of power that are so central to modern adversarial practices. It is a proposal for interaction that assists people to separate from impressive ways of speaking and that encourages people to situate their knowledges within the context of their lived experiences and their purposes.

Finally, it is a proposal for the privileging of embodied speech, not disembodied speech. They call for a version of dialogue that recognizes the complexity and the problematic nature of meaning-making, a version of dialogue that authorizes transparency and curiosity.

Haworth
DOCUMENT DELIVERY
SERVICE

This valuable service provides a single-article order form for any article from a Haworth journal.

- *Time Saving:* No running around from library to library to find a specific article.
- *Cost Effective:* All costs are kept down to a minimum.
- *Fast Delivery:* Choose from several options, including same-day FAX.
- *No Copyright Hassles:* You will be supplied by the original publisher.
- *Easy Payment:* Choose from several easy payment methods.

Open Accounts Welcome for . . .
- Library Interlibrary Loan Departments
- Library Network/Consortia Wishing to Provide Single-Article Services
- Indexing/Abstracting Services with Single Article Provision Services
- Document Provision Brokers and Freelance Information Service Providers

---

MAIL or *FAX* THIS ENTIRE ORDER FORM TO:

Haworth Document Delivery Service
The Haworth Press, Inc.
10 Alice Street
Binghamton, NY 13904-1580

or FAX: 1-800-895-0582
or CALL: 1-800-342-9678
9am-5pm EST

PLEASE SEND ME PHOTOCOPIES OF THE FOLLOWING SINGLE ARTICLES:
1) Journal Title: _____
   Vol/Issue/Year:_____Starting & Ending Pages:_____
   Article Title:_____
   _____

2) Journal Title: _____
   Vol/Issue/Year:_____Starting & Ending Pages:_____
   Article Title:_____
   _____

3) Journal Title: _____
   Vol/Issue/Year:_____Starting & Ending Pages:_____
   Article Title:_____
   _____

4) Journal Title: _____
   Vol/Issue/Year:_____Starting & Ending Pages:_____
   Article Title:_____
   _____

(See other side for Costs and Payment Information)

COSTS: Please figure your cost to order quality copies of an article.

1. Set-up charge per article: $8.00
             ($8.00 × number of separate articles)   _____

2. Photocopying charge for each article:
            1-10 pages: $1.00   _____

            11-19 pages: $3.00   _____

            20-29 pages: $5.00   _____

            30+ pages: $2.00/10 pages   _____

3. Flexicover (optional): $2.00/article   _____

4. Postage & Handling: US: $1.00 for the first article/
            $.50 each additional article   _____

            Federal Express: $25.00   _____

            Outside US: $2.00 for first article/
            $.50 each additional article   _____

5. Same-day FAX service: $.35 per page   _____

                      GRAND TOTAL: _____

METHOD OF PAYMENT: (please check one)

❏ Check enclosed   ❏ Please ship and bill. PO # _____
          (sorry we can ship and bill to bookstores only! All others must pre-pay)

❏ Charge to my credit card: ❏ Visa; ❏ MasterCard; ❏ Discover;
               ❏ American Express;

Account Number:_____ Expiration date:_____

Signature: ✗_____

Name: _____ Institution: _____

Address: _____

_____

City: _____ State:_____ Zip:_____

Phone Number: _____ FAX Number: _____

MAIL or *FAX* THIS ENTIRE ORDER FORM TO:

Haworth Document Delivery Service | **or FAX:** 1-800-895-0582
The Haworth Press, Inc. | **or CALL:** 1-800-342-9678
10 Alice Street | 9am-5pm EST)
Binghamton, NY 13904-1580